Saddle Up

A Cowboy Guide to Writing

To Inez,
all the best,
Slim Randles

SLIM RANDLES

Winner of the 2012 Rounders Award

Published by Rio Grande Books
Los Ranchos, New Mexico

Rio Grande Books

Rio Grande Books
Los Ranchos, New Mexico
www.LPDPress.com

Printed in the U.S.A.
Book design by Paul Rhetts
Cover art by Art Vincent
Illustrations by Ron Leishman: http://clipartof.com

Library of Congress Cataloging-in-Publication Data

Randles, Slim.
Saddle Up : a Cowboy Guide to Writing / by Slim
Randles.
pages cm
ISBN 978-1-936744-31-2 (pbk. : alk. paper)
1. Authorship--Handbooks, manuals, etc. 2. Au-
thorship--Vocational guidance. I. Title.
PN147.R37 2014
808.02--dc23
2013051003

For Kyra Lohuis, from her very lucky father

Foreword

In my many decades of living, working and reading in the great state of New Mexico, there is no one better than Slim Randles at writing 500 to 1,000 words. Slim has been a professional mule packer in the High Sierra of California. He has been a professional hunter and guide in the wilds of Alaska and New Mexico. Slim has taught writing at the university, and, more importantly, in person.

His early work with the *Albuquerque Journal* was truly magnificent, even though his territory was the farms, ranches and smaller towns surrounding Albuquerque. He spread his actual and innate knowledge in subjects from Louis l'Amour to a bull rider in Belen.

The multi-year columns in New Mexico Magazine, accompanied by Grem Lee's authentic and expert illustrations, are still imprinted on my mind and that of many others. Slim's sense of the tragedy and comedy of life was expertly done in every single issue.

Max Evans
Author of *The Rounders, Bluefeather Fellini*, and *The Hi-Lo Country.*

Introduction

"Slim's not back yet."

It was after dark in the Gila country and the entire elk camp was sitting around the fire.

"Yeah ….. he left early this morning to get the truck fixed in Reserve. Must've needed to get a part. He'll be back later tonight or tomorrow."

The sun rose and set on some wonderful elk country, but ….. another day with no Slim. The fire reflected off the camo faces of the concerned hunters.

"He must have had to wait to get a part shipped. If he's not back tonight or tomorrow by the time we get back to camp from the morning's hunt, we'll go find him."

Around 10 the next morning, everyone began to gather back in camp. The coffee was reheated and sipped but, Slim was still an absentee camp member.

"OK – let's grab a few snacks and head to town. It's time to find Slimbo. We'll get something to eat and pick up a few supplies too."

Within minutes, the crew was loaded in the truck and headed toward Reserve at near warp speed to solve the mystery. Our friend and hunting partner was still missing and we needed answers.

It was late morning when we arrived in Reserve and our renegade posse began prowling Main Street looking for the little Toyota truck or any tangible evidence of Slims whereabouts.

"There's the truck ..... over there by the motel and restaurant. "

We slowly crossed the street en mass (not unlike a group of Comancheros who have uncertain business in town) and cautiously entered the eatery.

As the door squeaked open we were greeted by riotous laughter and Slim's old Cowboy voice:

"SEE I TOLD YA - THEY'D COME AND FIND ME. CAMERE BOYS AND MEET MY NEW FRIENDS."

We had found Slim and he knew everyone in the restaurant by their first name. We extended a sincere howdy to all but especially to the motel and restaurant owner who had staked Slim to his short stay. Slim had not only thrown his back out when he got to town, but he'd forgotten his wallet and only had a few dollars tucked in his jeans. He had survived for over 2 days by doing what he does best: tell stories and make friends. It was a wonderful reunion and a great breakfast. After settling up, we sprung Slim and headed for greener pastures near the continental divide.

"I knew you guys would come and find me ......

That's what I kept telling Charlie. He trusted me and we sure had a good time visiting. My back sure was hurtin and I knew I couldn't make it back to camp so he put me up on my word and credit. Gee ….. what a nice group of people. We'll have to go back down and visit again before we leave. Say ……. How's Molly doing up in camp? I can't believe that guy drove into camp and called her a milk goat the other day ….. can you? Gee it's good to see you guys and get back to camp. Say …… did I ever tell you about the time Elmer Keith explained why the bighorn sheep were becoming scarce up in Idaho?" And so it goes. Ah……. the stories … the stories and the friendship.

I've traveled a few roads with Slim Randles and I've read every book he's written. I've even tracked down some of the hard to find works that he's penned (ghost written) while he achieved stature in his own right and I've been privileged to read some manuscripts before publication and offer an opinion. Now Slim has done a few things during his life; that goes without saying. But what he has done more than anything else, and what's been more important to him than anything else, is Writing with a capital W. He writes and that's why he has succeeded. His kit bag of experience includes reporting, editing, managing, lay-out, fiction, how to, biography and advice. And, he's done them all well.

Slim writes with an honesty that is not contrived. As a matter of fact, he's one of the most honest people I have ever met. Humorously, I often tell people by way of introducing Slim before they meet him that he's the guy I would like to lose my wallet in front of when it's filled with hundred dollar bills. Why, because I know without a doubt that it will be returned expeditiously and with everything intact. And, it will be returned graciously and without even a thought of reward. Why, because that's what people do for other people. His honesty is genuine in everything he does. So, when he gives you his best advice on writing and publishing: Listen up. Pay attention and work at the craft.

Slim's been writing professionally for over 50 years now and it's been my great honor to have hunted, fished and lived a few stories with him. Building memories and stories is what it's all about – isn't it? He's taken the next step though, he's brought those stories alive and entertained and informed countless people with his tales and insights. And, importantly, he's earned an honest living from his labors. Writing is hard work at times but if you have the desire and need to write, as Slim does, life can be a wonderful thing. Let's hope you heed his advice here and enjoy the fruits that are waiting to be plucked. Write well and honestly, and see where it leads you. I know where that road has taken Slim. And

….. I've been more than happy to tag along occasionally for the good times and ………. THE STORIES! Thanks amigo – for entertaining me and teaching me.

Dr. George L. Cornell
Professor and Director Emeritus
History and American Studies
and the Native American Institute
Michigan State University

ONE

Hey, anyone can be a writer!

Well, no they can't, actually. And – in a way – yes they can. Of course, if you made it through third grade, you probably know the basics to putting words on paper (or, these days, on a computer screen), but to actually reach out with words and communicate something to another human being, you'll need talent and training and experience.

A very famous novelist once told me "You should only be a writer if you have to."

There are easier ways of making a living, true. But if the idea of writing – for money – appeals to you, hang in here and let's see what we can do to help.

No they can't!

Let's look at this part first of our answer first.

I can't pick up a brush and oil paints and create something on canvas that other people enjoy seeing, but there are sure a lot of people who can. I can't sit down and put notes on music paper that orchestras can

1

turn into a wonderful, moving experience. My brother, Bob, can. I can't.

And not everyone can write. You know, Albert Schweitzer once said, "Setting an example isn't the best way to teach someone; it's the only way." That's good advice, so off and on, scattered through this book like Easter eggs in the backyard, I'll use my own, and other people's examples to show you what I mean.

Why, here's one of those now …

At one daily newspaper where I worked as a reporter, many years ago, we had a young guy who was one of the nicest people you could ever know. He had a degree in journalism from a large university, and was ready and eager to save the world by Tuesday at three o'clock.

He became the scourge of every bureaucrat trying to hide complicity in a no-no. He flew to the far corners of the state, gathering stories and interviewing people. He did a great job of it. But try as he might, he just couldn't write the story so it made any sense. He sweated blood over this. Everyone tried to help. Nothing worked. This was his dream, something he'd prepared himself for all through school, but when it came to making sense of all the facts he'd collected? Nothing.

So he became a "leg man." This used to happen more in newspapers back in the days of hot lead and "Hold page one!" and "Copy boy!" The paper sure didn't want to lose a good reporter like this just because he couldn't do the final ten percent of his job, so they'd send him out on a story and then he'd call someone in the newsroom designated as the "rewrite man" du jour, and give the rewrite all the facts. The rewrite would ask any questions of the reporter that seemed necessary at the time, such as "Was the senator crying at all when he said this?" And between the two of them, a pretty good story was born. We all took our turns being the rewrite man (or woman).

I often wonder where he is now and what he's doing. And I wonder why that journalism school gave him a diploma.

So … no. Not everyone can be a writer, sadly.

Yes they can!

Now let's have a peek at the flip side of this. Being a writer is one of those rare jobs that are open to anyone, as long as they have three things, in my opinion: 1. Basic talent, 2. A love of the language, and 3. A powerful curiosity.

Notice I didn't say 4. And have a burning message flaming deep within you to pour your guts out all over paper and show the world how smart you are.

If someday that should happen, super, but that's

not necessary to earning a living and having fun while writing things for publication.

But anyone? Yes. Editors and readers don't care how old or young you are. They don't care how much experience you've had or haven't had. They don't care how handsome or ugly you are. They don't care what race you are, what religion you practice, or what gender you are. (I write a syndicated newspaper column that appears in more than 200 papers each week, and at least half the editors are women). They don't care where you live or how much or how little money you make. They don't care if you are in a wheelchair, or even in prison. They don't care how much or how little education you have, as long as you can produce what they need, and do it well, and do it on time. Period.

Let's check out the three basics...

Talent. If you are a good letter writer, you'll probably be a good writer for everyone else.

If I may be permitted a personal aside here, I began trying to commit journalism at 15 by writing a column about rodeo cowboys for the local paper. But I'd stare at that blank paper and couldn't think of how to start it. So I would start each column by writing "Dear Mom" at the top. Shoot, I could write my mom a letter about this, after all. So when I finished, I went back and erased "Dear Mom" and sent the column in. Hey, whatever works.

A love of the language. It never ceases to amaze me how many people come up to me and say how everyone tells them they should write a book of their life someday, because it's been such a fascinating adventure. Hey, great. So what kind of books do you read? Oh, I don't have time for that.

This is akin to saying you really should build a house someday, but can't be bothered with learning how to swing a hammer and certainly aren't interested in reading plans

An insatiable curiosity. Actually, of the three, I'd sure put this at the top of the list. If you aren't dying to know why someone does something, or why an author wrote something just that way, or can't wait to learn how to take out someone's appendix, this writing business might not be right for you. If you read in the paper about somebody suddenly going bananas and shooting his neighbors, and you say to yourself "What in the world would make someone do something like that?" ... good.

You may say that a driving curiosity is certainly

required for being a reporter, but I want to be a WRITER! Well, that's fine, except that all writing is reporting. Let me repeat … ALL writing is reporting.

It is? Why, that's just nuts. Reporting is writing down what's going on. But my soul wants to soar ….!

There's no reason your soul can't get around to soaring. Hey, soaring is aces with me. And we'll get to soul soaring a bit later. But that doesn't change anything.

When Truman Capote wrote *In Cold Blood*, he was reporting – in a large and talented way, of course – on a family's murder in Kansas.

When Stephen Ambrose wrote *Band of Brothers*, he was reporting, in a very personal and brilliant kind of way, on World War II.

Sure, that's non-fiction. That really *is* reporting. But I'm interested in writing *fiction*. I want to make stuff up! My soul …

Yes, we know about your soul. So let's look at fiction. Fiction is simply reporting without having to check your facts.

Of course, when writing fiction, it's always good to know what you're talking about, so when you reach beyond your own limited experience, you're reporting. With fiction, you're reporting something that didn't happen. That's all. It's still reporting. You're telling the reader – in a brilliant and soaring way, of course – of something that should have, or shouldn't have, or could have, but didn't, happen.

(Okay, English teachers, let's see you parse *that* sentence!)

When a great science fiction writer like my neighbor, Robert Vardeman, for example, writes about stuff that didn't happen, might happen, might not happen, or whatever, he's reporting, too. But Bob is reporting on facts in a fictional world.

When a novelist writes about fictional folks, he is reporting on lives that didn't really happen, but need to be reported just the same.

Even with poetry and song. (Come on, Slim. That's nuts.)

When Robert W. Service wrote…

"Now Sam McGee was from Tennessee
Where the cotton blooms and blows…"

… he was reporting a situation, wasn't he? We learned a bit about Sam, and got a description of what Tennessee was like, but Service gave it to us in a lyrical, beautifully written poem.

And writing a song is simply reporting in poem form for some pal who has a guitar and can put chords to it and make it sound pretty.

It really is all a reporting job.

So let's have some fun and polish up the skills we have and make some money doing it.

TWO

Today's Magazine Market

You'll hear people talk, even today, about the Golden Age of Magazines. This was before television and computers, of course, back in the 1940s and 1950s. Ah, those days! We had the Big Guys then: *Life*, *Look*, *Time*, *Colliers*, *Atlantic Monthly*, and of course *The Saturday Evening Post*.

They paid big money for stories, and they attracted the best writers in the world.

And it was sure a lousy time to be starting out as a writer!

Why? Because, compared to today, you had very little chance of being considered seriously unless your last name was Hemingway, Fitzgerald, Ruark or Wolfe. It was a fairly small market and had thousands of people coming out of tough times in the Depression, and returning from the war with stories to tell, and things like construction and inventions were flourishing. And there were just a few magazines and each had only a few slots for freelance work in them.

To rub salt in the wound, most stories in each of these magazines were written by staff writers.

So how about today?

Hey, as I write this newspapers over 100 years old are closing. The economy is bad and advertising revenues are down. Computers and television are providing instant news to former newspaper readers. I'm in the newspaper business, these days as a syndicated columnist, and I specialize in providing columns for small-town weekly newspapers. These papers seem to be doing all right. These are still the papers that everyone buys to see how much the editor dared to print. But the large and medium-sized dailies are hurting.

But magazines are thriving. Fact: there are more magazines being published in the nation today than at any time in history. Fact: Most of them rely almost exclusively on freelance writers to "fill the book" each month.

Why?

Specialty-interest magazines. We get our fiction from other places these days. Our literature comes to us through books now, too. But we have hobbies and interests and more time on our hands to indulge ourselves. We like to read magazines with stories about our chosen field of work and our hobbies. Farmers can keep up on the latest in machinery, seed treatment, keeping books, milking machines and harvesting techniques in more than 20 magazines today.

It's pretty much the same no matter what your field of interest may be. Bob Petersen used to be the largest publisher of specialty-interest magazines in the world. Before he sold out, he had magazines on guns, cameras, hot rods, four-wheel-drive vehicles, motorcycles, hunting, camping and, at one time, hula hoops!

In the world of horses, there are not only dozens of magazines on horses, but magazines devoted to draft horses, cow horses, dressage horses, jumping horses, race horses, mules, and at least one magazine each for just about any breed of horse you can name.

The point is, each of these magazines, and hundreds more in other fields, has to have freelance stories to fill it up each month. So learn the correct way to do it, get published, get paid, and have fun.

THREE

Here's a short chapter you can read while making toast...

No one can teach you how to write

It's true, unfortunately. And fortunately.

A skilled bricklayer can teach you how to lay bricks. There is a right way and a wrong way to do it. There are a lot of jobs like that, but writing isn't one of them. There is no right way or wrong way to write.

Well, the wrong way would be to put the reader to sleep, of course, but if you can keep him awake and alert and interested, you can pretty much do it any way you like.

I know there are journalism teachers (and university English professors) who claim they'll teach you how to write. Then they tell you how *they* write, and yours had better sound like theirs when you're done. Most professional writers – including this one – aren't quite that cocky or self-assured. We know how *we* do it. You're free to pursue developing your own "voice." In fact, we think it's a grand idea.

Example: which one of these was a great writer, Hemingway or Shakespeare?

Answer: Both (of course). But they sure didn't write alike, did they? And I'll bet you can be given a random paragraph from either one and tell which one wrote it.

So there isn't one way to write. There are thousands or maybe millions of ways to write. And you could very well add your own voice to the list.

No one can teach you how to write, but we can do other things.

A coach or teacher can take what you've written and suggest ways of making it better. We can advise you on what to put in and what to leave out. We can advise you on words to use that could carry more punch than the ones you used in the first draft. We can act as a cheering section when you feel inadequate (and you will), and when your work is rejected (oh yes, that will happen, too).

And we can tell you about other people and how they handle the writing game, and I can tell you stories from the half century now that I've spent attempting to commit journalism.

Hopefully, these will make up for not being able to teach you how to write.

FOUR

The three universal truths in publishing ...

1. Turn in clean copy, on time, and you'll get checks in the mail.

You might want to have someone handy carve that into a wooden plaque and hang it above your desk. Well, remember it anyway, okay?

2. Editors and publishers only want to work with professional writers.

You might want to have someone handy ... oh, we already said that with the first U.T.

3. Make life easy for an editor and you'll always have work.

Especially ditto on this one. Maybe carve it on an oak two by six. It'll last longer.

Let's take these one at a time and check them over. At first they may seem to be in the "Well, duh" department of universal truths. You know, self-evident, etc. But these are the three things most beginning writers get wrong, and it can come back to bite them in the butt on down the road. So let's get it right … right now. Saves all that wailing and gnashing of teeth later on.

Turn in clean copy…

Before you send something off to an editor or publisher, be it a short piece for the paper or a monumental novel where your soul soars, have someone else read it.

But, you say, I'm really good at spelling and punctuation and grammar. Hey, I went to grammar school!

I'm really good at that stuff, too. Always have been, as a matter of fact. So why do I have someone else read my stuff before any stamps are affixed (or we push the Send button)? Because it's always better to have another set of eyes look at it first. My wife, Catherine, is really good at catching little screw-ups and I really enjoy having her look things over. Also, however, she's an avid reader. So if she puts a question mark by a sentence and says, "I'm not sure what you're trying to say here," I say "THANK YOU!"

Because if she, or your wife, or the friendly grocer or your oldest kid has to ask you to clarify something, that's absolutely terrific. That means go back and fix it.

But let's say spelling and grammar and whether to

use a colon or semicolon is not your strong suit. Should this prevent you from selling good stories and moving along toward some serious soul soaring later? Of course not.

That's why God made English teachers.

I'm not going to name a name here, but I will tell you from absolute personal experience that one of the icons in one field of writing, with more than a dozen books and hundreds of magazine articles to his credit was functionally illiterate.

If you read his monthly column in the magazine, you could sometimes tell which of the in-house editors had done the rewrite. Sometimes he'd sound like a professor of philosophy and sometimes like a good ol' boy. So why would a publisher bother with someone so ill-suited to be a writer? Because this guy was an acknowledged expert in his chosen field, and he could tell a good story.

So how do I know this? I ghost-wrote his autobiography from a shoebox full of cassette tapes. I made him sound like a good ol' boy. Which he was.

So if you're a good storyteller and really want to be a writer, this is not an impossibility. It just takes more work.

Let me tell you about one of my closest pals over the last 40 years. I won't name him, either, because he's sensitive about this. He wrote a novel, a Western, and had it subsidy published, which means basically he paid a printer to make a book out of it. They were going to charge him a lot of money to do the copy editing on this, so he skipped that part.

Well, my ol' pard is a terrific storyteller, but his spelling and grammar and punctuation are for the birds. I mean, really bad. And I told him that.

He's in the midst of writing novel number two as I write this, and is planning to take some high school English classes in the spring. This takes guts for a man who has been retired for several years now and I admire him greatly.

So novel number one has now gone to a professional rewrite person for a thorough tune-up, and then it will be submitted by my buddy to a real publisher for consideration. He'll do the same thing with novel number two. This will cost him several hundred bucks per book, because there's a whole bunch of work to be done, but it will be worth it. Why?

Because he can sure tell a great yarn.

English teachers are a lot more common than good storytellers, and many of them can use the extra bucks.

So turn in clean copy. Ready to go. If you make life easy for an editor …

Oh, that's number three. We'll get to that in a minute.

Turn in your story on time …

This sounds pretty stupid at first, because it seems so obvious. But it isn't obvious to people just getting into the writing field, so it bears a few minutes of explanation.

When you send an editor a query letter (we'll deal with those in the next chapter), a strong part of the letter will be a date when the story can be on the editor's desk. This applies whether it's a short piece for a magazine, or the Great American Non-fiction book or even a novel. Why? Because publishing is a business. They manufacture a product. They want to publish good stuff, on time, and make a profit. If they don't … they'll be unemployed and their dog will starve. So it's important to tell them when the story or book can be on their desk, and then make sure it is.

If you know for an absolute fact that you can have that magazine article on the editor's desk by May, tell him he'll have it by June. Then get it on his desk by May. He'll think you're a ball of fire and will give you more work.

Why is this important? Magazines are put together months before you get yours in the mail, sometimes six months or even longer before you get them. The editor has to plan for these issues. If you tell him (or her) you can have that piece on how to extract vitamins from swamp water at the magazine by June, he can then say to himself, "Well, I'll be putting the November issue together then, so to leave myself some slack, I'll figure on it for the December issue."

What happens when someone doesn't deliver on time? Well, in one case, I was called by the editor of one of the largest outdoor magazines in existence and asked if I could write a piece on being attacked by grizzly bears and get it to him in two days. Said he'd pay me twice the going rate if I could pull it off. I sent it to him the next day. He thinks I'm great.

What happened here? Well, some guy was attacked by a grizzly bear and lived through it and he told the editor he'd write the story and have it to him at a certain time. So the editor put a photo of a grizzly – complete with open mouth and fangs – in glorious color on the COVER along with a cover blurb (a teaser) saying something like "I Survived a Grizzly Attack!"

Then they never heard from the bear's victim again. Now these covers are usually printed up a month or so ahead of the inside of the magazine, as a lot of them are done overseas because of cost, and because they have to do them in color, which means running it through a special press four different times and it takes longer and the printers have to fiddle with it a bunch to get it right.

So here's the editor with a cover that would make a homicide detective wet the bed, and no story.

Actually, I have never been eaten by a grizzly bear, despite having given the rascals several opportunities (hey, that's why hunting guides like me carry rifles). But fortunately I knew a number of people who had been attacked, and put a piece together for the magazine.

Two things happened here.

1. I get more work from the magazine. These things become known.

2. The guy who got chomped will probably never write for another magazine again. These things become known, too.

I realize you believe fervently that the editor can't wait to read your story, and you should probably FedEx it to him immediately to quell the burning curiosity in his soul, but that isn't what's going on. He doesn't care when you get it to him, as long as he can count on it being there then.

So when you tell an editor the date he can have your piece, give yourself lots of margin. Hey, you could get sick, you could be invited to visit China, you could win the Nobel Prize and have to go to Sweden and eat meatballs. Things happen.

But if you are reliable and on time, you'll get work.

Be a professional writer …

… because editors and publishers only want to work with professional writers. Professionals make life easy for an editor and therefore get the assignments and get space in the magazine and their books get larger advance payments against royalties.

But – you wail through the gnashing of teeth – I'm not a professional! I'm just starting!

Easy there, pard. Remember the last chapter? You can be a writer no matter how experienced or inexperienced you are. Why? Because you don't tell them this is your first story. Not unless they ask. And they won't. In fact, they don't care!

If you approach them in a professional manner (query letter, etc.) they will assume you're a pro and have been doing this for years. In many years of doing this, I've never had a magazine editor ask me for a resume' or a list of magazines I've written for. Ever. You won't either. Why would they?

If you turn in clean copy on time and use a query letter, you are a pro. Period.

Make an editor's life easy and you'll get work … and money

An editor's life can be very stressful. They worry a lot. Some of them take little pills. There are nasty things called deadlines that mess with a guy's nervous system. I've been associate editor of a national magazine, editor and publisher of two small papers in Alaska, and managing editor of a daily paper in Texas. I know.

So if you learn how an editor wants to be approached, and approach him that way, you'll get work. If you turn in clean copy on time, and the story has the ingredients the editor asked for, you'll get work.

An editor I was working for once on a magazine walked into my office waving an envelope and saying "I think I just fell in love!"

Well, the writer he fell in love with was another guy, in a tiny town in Wyoming, and we'd never heard of him before, but he'd queried, got what we call a go-ahead from the editor (more on that later) and delivered. On time.

"Look at this," the editor said. "He has photographs of animals, facing left and facing right. He has rifle line-ups, left and right. He has a cartridge line-up. The story's perfect and I don't have to change a word. He wrote a sidebar on what the hunting licenses cost and how to get them. I tell you, I'm in love!"

That first-time writer became a household name in outdoor publishing. That particular story was on how to successfully hunt antelope in Wyoming. He had asked a professional writer how to approach a magazine and was told.

(A little explanatory aside here may be helpful regarding the goodies that came with that story. A line-up is when you have a photo of four or five rifles that would be useful in taking an antelope. The cartridge line-up is the same. Popular calibers for antelope. The facing left and facing right part is important because you can't have guns – or cars or people or antelope – pointing off the page. They have to point toward the binding. So if the editor gets one to the left and one to the right, he doesn't have to fret over whether to put the picture on a right-hand page or a left-hand page. A sidebar is usually one of those little boxes that get stuck in the story that gives the reader more information. Magazines use them a lot in suggesting hotels to stay in, hiking trails nearby, who rents sailboats, things like that. And for a bonus on your climb up the journalistic ladder, if you can think of a sidebar the editor hadn't even thought of when you got the go-ahead, and you go ahead and put it in there, you could have someone fall in love with you, too!)

FIVE

Personal note – This chapter will pay you for buying the whole book. If we had pop quizzes, you'd get one at the end of this chapter.

Sell it BEFORE you write it!

How do you do that? By using a query letter. With the exception of the local weekly (or daily) paper, where they have telephones, this is standard procedure for magazines and especially for books. And it has even been used, in rare cases, for novels.

How I got started …

I wanted to be a writer. I wanted to write for a magazine. So I thought up a story that would be in line with that magazine's needs (in this case, horses) and I researched it and wrote it. Then I put it in a big envelope with a self-addressed stamped envelope, and mailed it, with fingers crossed, to the editor.

In a couple of months, I got my story back with a printed rejection slip saying "Thank you for your submission to *Horsin' Around Magazine*. Unfortunately, your submission does not fit our needs at this time."

Of course, being an eternally optimistic teenager at the time, I just thought "Wow! They thanked me for sending it! I'll have to do that again."

I was so darn dumb I even wrote a piece on rodeo cowboys and mailed it to *Atlantic Monthly*!

Why? Because they paid more money for stories than Horsin' Around did.

So I got another rejection slip, but this time from a magazine that paid five times as much as the last one! And, being a skinny, idiot cowboy, I thought that was progress.

As it turned out, by the time I built that cabin in Alaska, I could've wallpapered the place with rejection slips.

That is not how you become a writer. Don't do it that way.

That method of story submission does accomplish several things, however. 1. It costs you postage and envelope money, 2. It wears out the mailman, 3. It makes several editors wish they'd never heard your name, and 4. It's really depressing and leads to thoughts like "I'm not a good writer, so maybe I should just clean corrals or teach at the university."

So the way to avoid all this rejection and the waste of days of time writing things no one wants to publish is to only write the things people *want* to publish. And we do that by using the query letter.

Let's take a look at this from the other guy's point of view for a minute.

Here's the scene ....

You are editor of a magazine. You walk into your office in the morning and head for the coffee pot. Taking your cup of eye-opener, you head to the desk, and what do you find? A stack of six or seven big, fat manila envelopes with completed stories and snapshots from people you don't know. And one skinny letter.

You have about ten minutes before you have to get to work on the April issue (it's now about Thanksgiving time) so which of these envelopes should you open over coffee? The skinny one. Why? Because it's a query letter from a professional writer. How do you know it's a professional writer if you don't recognize the return address? Because sending a one-page query letter is what professionals do.

You open it, read it, and if the story idea inside (on taking care of goldfish) is something you might be interested in, you pick up the phone, call the writer, and say something like "I'd be interested in looking at a story on taking care of goldfish. Maybe 1,000 words? Can you emphasize how much to feed them? Okey doke. Thanks for thinking of us." Click.

That's what is called a "go-ahead." Notice the editor said he'd be interested in *looking* at a piece. This leaves him an out, you see. If it turns out that the goldfish story you send him isn't written well, he can always reject it and say it didn't fit whatever needs they have. He's not committing himself to buying it. But at this point, rejecting it almost never happens. Why not? Because 1. By querying him you have proven yourself to be a professional, and he needs professional writers in order to "fill the book" with stories every month. And 2. You have already gotten past 90 per cent of the reasons for being rejected.

Why is a story rejected?

1. You already wrote it and put it in the mail to him, and the story didn't emphasize how much to feed the little rascals and the story is about 2,000 words longer than he wanted.

2. You already wrote it, thus proving to him that you are not a professional writer and therefore violating a Universal Truth.

3. He just bought a piece which will run in the March issue on caring for goldfish and it emphasizes how much to feed them.

4. Your story wasn't well written.

Number Four is at the end, because that's almost never the case. It's those first three that will kill your story. Every time.

Give an editor what he wants and you'll get work. And the editor wants a query letter.

So what is a query letter?

It's a story idea. Period.

You see, the magazine (and we'll discuss book queries later) is a monthly product. It is like a buffet for the reader. It has stories on a variety of subjects, and most magazines have a … well, a formula, I guess. A blending. At my old alma mater, *Petersen's Hunting*, for example, each month we had a story on small game, big game, bow hunting, exotic game (African safari stuff), upland bird hunting, hunting waterfowl, and field tests on new guns and gear. You know, try to put something in there for everyone who is interested in hunting.

Almost all magazines have a similar blend, which you can discover by going down to the drug store and buying a copy. Now there's a radical idea. See what they have. See those stories? They *paid* for those stories. That's the kind of story they want in the magazine. Notice about how long each piece is. Do they use stock photos or will you be expected to take some? Do they illustrate the stories with drawings from the staff artist?

Offer something they might like

You look at a couple of months' worth of the magazine you're interested in and then send in an idea that fits what they use. You don't query *Hunting Magazine* on a piece called "Catching Rainbow Trout in Montana." Look at the name of the magazine. Yep, a fishing query would be a waste of your time and the editor's time.

This would also very likely not be the place to send in a story on why you are a vegetarian.

Use your head on these things before you query.

Let's look at a silly sample of what I consider a decent query letter.

Sample Magazine Query Letter

Quentin Slaymore, editor
Love That Serpent Magazine
Squeaky Moccasin, WY

Dear Mr. Slaymore:

Bobby Blake was just a month shy of his 12th birthday that beautiful autumn day in the Wisconsin woods, and had no idea it was to be his last day on earth. Bobby fell victim to the rare but deadly Wisconsin carpet viper, one of our lesser-known rural killers.

Overshadowed by the more abundant rattlesnakes and water moccasins on the list of crawling assassins, the Wisconsin carpet viper nevertheless manages to kill an average of five hikers each year from the protection of its camouflaging leaf litter. The deaths come despite warnings on how to avoid places the snakes like, and some straightforward methods of treating the rare bites.

I have no photos of this snake, but there are a number available from the Wisconsin Department of Natural Resources. A story on this unusual snake can be on your desk in 60 days.

Thank you for your time,

Slender Slither
(505) 555-1234
sslither@write.em.com
235 Elm Street
Truth or Consequences, NM

(First of all, there isn't a Wisconsin carpet viper, so don't cancel your trip to Madison.)

This query letter has a number of things included in it, and a whole bunch of things not included in it, and it could very well be that the things that aren't included are more important. Let's look at what 'ol Slender put in this letter.

1. Most importantly – phone number and email address. The editor has to know how to get you instantly.

2. It's very short.

3. A sample of your writing that shows him you can write and that you understand what a catchy lead is on a story. That's what the first two sentences do for you, and for him. (Two sentences. Three. tops. Don't beat him to death with it.)

4. It all fits on one side of a piece of paper.

5. It shows the editor several different directions the story could take. Such as a. first aid for a bite, b. where in the woods these snakes are found, and c. how to avoid being bitten.

6. It's short.

7. It tells him when he can expect the story.

8. It's not very long.

9. It fills him in on the photo possibilities. You don't have to have the photos yourself, but he appreciates knowing where he might find some if you should know. A couple of phone calls should give you an idea of where to find them, and will save him the time and he'll appreciate it.

10. It takes only seconds to read it.

Got it? Good.

Now let's look at what this query letter does not have in it.

1. Lots and lots of words.

2. How long your story is. Why not? Because you haven't written it yet! Professional writers sell a piece before they write it.

3. A lot of words describing just how this story of yours has been designed, and listing a corral full of footnotes on scholarly snake books you've read. He doesn't care.

4. A lot of words telling the editor about you. He doesn't care.

5. A long dissertation based on why you find snakes fascinating. He doesn't care, as long as you can write for people who do find snakes fascinating.

6. Eighteen reasons why you should be the one to write this story. You have a doctorate in herpetology, a masters in using a snake bag, a bachelor's in hissing. He doesn't care. You don't have to be an expert. You are a reporter. Go find an expert, then report.

7. How much your wife and the neighbor guy enjoyed reading it. You haven't written it yet, remember?

8. How easy or difficult it will be for you to get this story. He doesn't care.

9. How you can have it to him tomorrow if he'd like.

(He'll know you've already written it.)

Of course, this will be *your* story. You'll want to do the best you can with it and give it a real polish and make it sing. Remember that, in most cases, you'll be known only by the stories you produce. So make them good. But the reason you give the editor a number of ways to go with the piece is because it's *his* magazine. The whole magazine is his baby, and he wants it to reflect him. So let him steer you in the right direction and let him tell you how long he'd like it.

Editors have likes and dislikes, just like the rest of us, so give him what he needs to turn out an issue he can proudly say is in his own image.

Let me tell you a little story about Gibb and Stan, two of my buddies from the old days on the *Anchorage Daily News.*

Gibb was managing editor. Stan was executive editor. The bosses.

But each of us has pet peeves and pet fascinations and pet likes. They were no exception. Gibb loved sea otters. He could tell you all about them. We picked up a wire story one day about how a zoo in California didn't have the right salinity in the water in the sea otter tank and a couple of otters went to Heaven over it. The rage was on. "Just see if I send THEM any more #@$%& sea otters!" Gibb raved.

Of course, Gibb had never sent a sea otter to anyone and had absolutely no say in it, but that didn't quell the newsroom meltdown.

Now Stan was there in Anchorage for the Big Earthquake of 1964. It was rumored that a building's wall had fallen on his new sports car. He hated earthquakes. If you accidentally bumped his desk, he was out in the street. When we actually did have an earthquake, which seemed like every other week up there, Stan would fly into action, designating reporters to find out what the thing scored on the Richter Scale, where the epicenter was, who lived close to the epicenter and could give us a blow-by-blow look at how many dishes fell out of the cupboard, and call the fire department and see if it caused any stores to blow up.

He hated them.

So one day a story came in about the military wanting to set off an underground nuclear blast on Amchitka Island in the Aleutians. This happened to be the home of a huge coagulation of sea otters and was on the junction of two major earthquake faults. You should've read the editorials in the *Daily News*!

My point here? Everyone has his pet peeves, just like Gibb and Stan. Every editor has subjects they enjoy dwelling on and others that put them to sleep.

If you read the magazines, you can pretty much figure out what those are after a while, and use it to your advantage.

Give him what he wants and you'll get checks in the mail.

Got it? Good.

We'll get into query letters for books a bit later on, because they need more stuff, but a magazine story doesn't.

Now if you're ol' Quent Slaymore at the magazine up in Wyoming and you get this letter from Mr. Slither about Wisconsin carpet vipers, you'll sip your coffee and think for a minute. We haven't had a piece on the carpet viper in several years. Maybe it's time to have another look at the snake. Or ... we had a carpet viper piece last year, but it really didn't go into first aid for a bite. If Slender doesn't mind handling it that way, maybe he could interview a doctor or something and this could work for us. I think I'll give him a call.

Or ... I don't need a piece on carpet vipers, but this guy is obviously a pro, and I've heard of a rare green rattlesnake that supposedly lives within 100 miles of him. I think I'll call and see if he can do a piece on that.

That, dear reader, is how it works.

Sell the story *before* you write it.

SIX

Building a reputation through query letters

One of the strangest – and truest – things that can happen in publishing is that you can actually build a good reputation as a writer without ever actually writing a story. How is that possible?

Just through the liberal use of good query letters. Of course, you want the editor to bite the bait and give you the go-ahead ... every time. But even if your letters don't exact the desired response, there is a wonderful thing that happens. Every politician knows this: name recognition.

Why do you think politicians put up signs that just have their names on them? Most of them don't say which party they belong to and none of them tell you why you should vote for them. They're just up there so if you drive by often enough before election day, you'll see the name on the ballot and say "I've heard of this guy" and vote for him.

I'm not suggesting you flood editors with query letters. Far from it. Never write a query letter you aren't prepared to back up with a good story ... on time.

But professional writers are a rarity compared to the stories that come in "over the transom."

Trivia Break!

("Over the transom" is an interesting expression meaning the editor didn't ask for them. Back when offices had above-the-door transoms, a bulky envelope – such as a manuscript – was tossed over the transom into the office by the mailman because it wouldn't fit through the mail slot in the door. You didn't know that? You're welcome. No extra charge.)

This rarity of pro writers strikes a real chord with editors. Maybe your piece on goldfish isn't for them, but they'll probably send you a note or email rather than a rejection slip. Something personal and friendly. Why? Because they'll want to hear from you again with another story idea.

And what happens? Your name will be stored away in the old editor's cerebral cortex. The next time he sees your name, he might not remember the goldfish query, but he associates your name with "professional writer" and with a pleasant experience. That's not a bad deal.

Follow Grandma Post's advice …

She always used to say, "Now don't overdo it!" She

wasn't referring to query letters, but it's still good advice. One of the questions I always get when speaking to writing groups is "How many query letters should I send out on a story?"

Whoa, Nellie!

Can you back each one of them up with a story ... on time? You should never "shotgun" query letters, anyway. By that I mean changing only the editor's name and address on the query and sending it to every magazine that might be interested in the piece. This is a real temptation for beginning writers and is the journalistic equivalent of throwing a mud ball against a wall and hoping some of it sticks. It's actually something close to journalistic suicide.

Let's say you bounce the goldfish care idea off one magazine and you don't hear from back from the editor. How much time should you give him before you give up and send the idea to another magazine? I think two weeks is plenty of time. That is enough time to be courteous and to offer exclusive rights to the goldfish idea. And isn't that a whole lot better than sending off an unsolicited manuscript and waiting months to hear back?

I would sure suggest keeping a chart or something so you know the status of every query letter and story you write. I'm not, by nature, an organized guy. Seriously.

So I have to force myself to be organized. Hopefully, you're a lot better at keeping track of things than I am.

Being a freelance magazine writer is akin to being a juggler and having five or six balls in the air at the same time.

"Sequential exclusivity" is a phrase I just made up. (Wouldn't that be a great name for a race horse? "Rounding the clubhouse turn, it's ...) It means one editor at a time. Give that editor enough time to either say no thanks or to give you a go-ahead. Some writers will disagree that two weeks is enough time to give editors to respond to a well-written query letter. Hey, this is America. They're entitled to be wrong.

So how long should you wait before sending this editor another query letter on a different story idea? There are no rules on this, of course, but I'd give it a month. You don't want to be a pest.

Of course, one of the half-dozen or so pet fish magazines will take you up on that goldfish piece and you'll write it and get paid for it and it'll show up on down the road. So the first editor ... the one who said no thanks ... will see the piece in the rival magazine and the name will ring a bell. Oh ... professional writer. Friendly memory. Wish he'd send me something.

And the editors of "*Tetra Today*," "*Gourami Gazette*," and the other fish mags will see it, too, because they all read the competition. Every month. And there's your piece in "*Aquarium Age*" to impress them. So what happens?

The next time one of your query letters hits their desk, they're going to try really hard to either find room for that story, or to call you and suggest another. Hey, these people need your stories!

World's shortest career in magazine writing …

… was experienced by a bow hunter, many years ago, who was pursuing elk in Colorado and was mauled by a bear, which he fatally wounded with an arrow. Stabbed it to death. True story. So he wrote it up and sent it off.

Now which outdoor magazine editor could pass up a story like this? His story on the episode came in over the transom and was published … simultaneously … by five outdoor magazines!

Word for word. Identical stories. Identical photos of the dead bear. Three of the magazines used it for cover art, too.

I was sitting at my desk, going over the rival magazines and seeing this same story, by the same guy, in the competition. "Hey," I said to publisher Ken Elliott (*Hunting Magazine*), "look at this! Some guy sold the same story to a bunch of magazines."

Ken looked at it and said, "Boy, I'm glad I didn't buy

that story." Yep, he'd sent it to *Hunting*, too.

If this guy was hoping for a career as an outdoor writer, he'd have to wait until every editor on every outdoor magazine died of old age. We haven't heard from him since.

Grandma Post would say he definitely overdid it.

Querying on a new slant …

Now there is a way of spreading story ideas out into multiple pieces in multiple magazines, and doing it "legally" and acceptably.

Let's take the goldfish idea here and see what we can do with it.

We've decided that pet fish is our field of interest. We want to write about fish in tanks. There are half-a-dozen magazines in the field. This is probably true no matter what your particular field of interest is, by the way.

We've just sent off a query to *"Aquarium Age"* on how much to feed goldfish and we're waiting to hear. So are we just going to bask in the sun on the Riviera sipping an adult beverage until we hear back?

Of course not. So we query *"Tetra Today"* on a piece about how to monitor the freshness of the water. We query *"Angel Fish Forum"* on new trends in aquarium pumps. And we query *"Gourami Gazette"* on the ages-old question - To Flush, or Not to Flush, when the inevitable end comes and our little finny pals go belly up.

See how that works?

And if the editor of "*Aquarium Age*" passes on the feeding goldfish story, we're then free to offer that idea to "*Tropical Fish Times*."

And of course we keep scrupulous track of who was sent what, and when. It wouldn't do our reputations any good to send the same query letter to an editor twice, would it? And we've made certain, in every query letter we send out, that we've left ourselves enough time to fulfill each of these story ideas if they all say go ahead at the same time!

Remember: the active ingredient in the word "deadline" is "dead." Don't blow it.

One other note here – if you're a first-timer with a magazine, and the editor gives you a go-ahead on a story, write that story and get it in to him before querying him again on another piece. He'll want to know what you can do and that you can do it on time before considering a second story. Of course, once you're established with editors, you won't need to worry about that any more.

SEVEN

Meet *Writer's Market*

So just how do you go about getting addresses for all these magazines and book publishers?

For the best part of a century now, there has been a big, fat book called *Writer's Market*. Inside *Writer's Market* is almost every publication, here and abroad, along with book publishers and play producers. Each magazine has the name of the editor, how they'd like to be approached (query letter, completed manuscript, etc.), the kinds of stories they like, about how long the stories should be, and how much and when they pay.

This monster book is updated each year, and the year is printed right on the cover so you know you're getting the latest edition. It'll list all the like subjects together: aviation magazines here, horse magazines there, markets for fiction over here, etc. This way, if you want to submit recipes, all the cooking magazines will be bunched up.

You can certainly buy this book, but it tends to be pretty expensive, and in 12 months it'll be outdated.

But the secret is, almost every public library in the country has a copy. They're considered reference books so chances are you can't check it out, but you can sit there and make notes for hours, if you want to.

It's an excellent resource. And I think you'll be amazed at how many different markets there are for your work. I was, and I still am.

So you trip over an entry in *Writer's Market* that says it's all right to send in a completed manuscript for them to look at. This would be in the magazine department, I mean, not in books. Books are a different deal.

Should you send the magazine a completed manuscript? Suit yourself, but I wouldn't. Why go to all the trouble of writing and polishing something only to have it rejected? So for the few magazines that will tell you this, I'd still query them first.

Most all magazines will say "query first." Do it.

Code words:

You'll run across sentences like these in *Writer's Market*: 1. We accept no unsolicited manuscripts. 2. We accept no unagented manuscripts.

An unsolicited manuscript is a completed story that comes in over the transom. A solicited manuscript is one where the editor has given you a go-ahead after you queried him.

An unagented manuscript is used much more with books than with magazine stories, but it will crop up from time to time. In my never-humble opinion, a magazine that demands an agent send them a story is both lazy and putting on airs.

They want a professional (the agent) to screen it for them, for free, before they get it. Saves them time and money. As far as looking down their noses at writers and saying "You peons have to get someone with an education to send this to me." Well, any editor who would do that would steal sheep.

Should you have an agent? Yes and no. We'll look at that now.

EIGHT

Do I need an agent?

No you don't. Hey, it's great fun (and a convenience) to have one, but necessary? No.

In the first place, it's harder'n sin to get one. Finding an agent who will believe in you and your work and knock themselves out for you is one of the great Catch 22 situations the world has ever seen, leading us to yet another Universal Truth.

U.T. – You can only get an agent when you don't need one.

Yes. It's only when you are an established, successful writer that an agent will be interested in representing you. Why waste all your agenting expertise on an unknown? It does make sense, of course.

I have had the same agent now for the past 25 years, Destiny Marquez of Marqcom Media. On a handshake. Well, more on a hug, really. She's one of my closest friends and she'll be my agent until they pry my keyboard from my cold, dead fingers.

But I was already an established newspaper columnist when I met her, and had already had three books published, as well as several hundred magazine articles.

If an agent isn't necessary, why bother to have one? Well, I'd rather spend my time writing than selling, for one thing. Also, she knows a bunch about movie contracts and options and New York publishers and I'm tickled pink to let her mess with them.

So many new writers come to me and tell me they're trying to find an agent before they write *The Book*. I always suggest they wait until after *The Book III* is successful before looking for an agent.

Don't waste time agent hunting. It'll take time away from your writing.

NINE

The Art of the Interview

Permit me a little snippishment here (don't you love inventing words?) If you turn on the television any weekday morning and see people well-coiffed and smiling and talking to each other, you would certainly know all about interviewing someone.

The person being interviewed would be someone in the news, so we don't need background but go directly to the big question: "Governor, how did that make you *feel*?"

But for those of us who think as well as feel, interviewing is an art form that can be learned and polished over years of trial and error. This chapter can be considered a shortcut that will knock a few years off the trial-and-error period.

Why the interview?

I don't care what you're writing, the interview should become a vital member of the arrows in your writing quiver. If you're a newspaper reporter, of course, it's something you use almost every day. If you're a freelance for magazines, this craft or art of interviewing is essential. Why? Because no matter what the subject is, there is someone, somewhere, who is an expert in that subject and has knowledge to impart.

As an editor, the interview was something I couldn't get enough of. I'll bet any magazine editor will tell you the same thing. If your specialty-interest magazine deals with tropical fish, learn who invented the circulating filter, for Pete's sake, and ask for an interview.

If you write for cars, televisions or computers, the technology happens every day. Interview someone who is on the cutting edge of your chosen field. Remember: you don't have to be an expert in the field. You're a reporter. Find someone who is an expert and report.

And then there are the celebrities. These are fun. Whether it's the author of a string of best sellers, a sports legend or a movie star, it's kinda cool to add these to your personal treasure chest. My own personal treasure chest, for example, includes Louis L'Amour, Joe DiMaggio and Roy Rogers. Really fun.

As an interviewer, you can have access to these people. Why? Because they didn't become celebrities by telling reporters to go take a hike. This is their stock in trade.

(A little personal philosophical aside here: When I

lived in Hollywood, it never ceased to amaze me that up-and-coming entertainers would rent billboards to spread their smiles all over town to become known, and then, when success hits, drive a car with smoked-glass windows so no one can see it's really them. People are funny.)

Thanks for allowing me the occasional philosophical aside. Makes it more fun for me, you see. There will be more.

So to summarize, I can't think of a single magazine that doesn't need interviews. People are interested in other people. People with a certain hobby, such as making custom knives, are fascinated by the big names in the field, such as Gerber, Randall and Cordova.

How about books? Interviews for books? Sure.

Non-fiction and fiction? You bet.

How many times do you think Tom Wolfe personally flew jet planes faster than sound before writing The Right Stuff? Yet he found out how it was done, didn't he?

How many submarines do you think Tom Clancy drove before he was qualified to write The Hunt for Red October? Get the picture?

For my novel, The Long Dark, for instance, I needed to know what goes on in the cockpit of a Boeing 737 jet liner, so I was lucky enough to track down a friendly airline pilot and pick his brain.

So for books, magazines, movies, and newspapers, the interview's the thing. Take advantage of it and learn it well. When all else fails in the world of being a freelance writer, this one will put money in your pocket.

So how do I learn?

Well, you're making a good start by reading this chapter, of course. But there are other ways to hone these skills. If you're just starting out as a writer, my advice would be to go to the local newspaper and offer your services for a few interviews. Should you get paid for it? I wouldn't even bring the subject up. It's always nice to be paid, and if it happens, super. But this is for your education, isn't it? You wouldn't expect Harvard University to pay you to sit in a chemistry class, would you?

Look around you. Whether you're in a tiny farming town or a big city, it won't be hard to find someone to interview. If you're in a big city, look for the radicals. I mean that in a loving fashion, too. There are always those out there who see the world through really different lenses than the rest of us. They are always interesting and always eager for ink.

I once covered a fairly routine story about the county agriculture extension guy taking gardeners out in the field and showing them how to slay gophers to protect their asparagus.

Holy Crow! How was I to know there's a Save the Gopher group? I heard all about it.

And interviewing the gopher saver made a much more interesting piece than the extension guy.

That's what I mean by radical. Look for someone interesting and different, who may have different ideas than most of us. We really enjoy reading things that have headlines that say, "Harmon says gophers are essential."

I'd guess that sounds more interesting than a headline that declares "Gophers can ruin your garden."

Look for characters

Everyone loves to read about what we call characters. You know, the old sidewalk philosophers, the lady who feeds red ants in her yard, the retired corporation president who volunteers as a crossing guard at the elementary school, the old lady who swears she can cure carbuncles with iron water and celery roots.

So how do you find them?

Consult the local research library of all things weird: bartenders, barbers, beauticians and truck-stop waitresses.

A simple question like "Who's the strangest person

you've ever served?" should take care of the problem. And every newspaper editor I've ever known loves these stories. And please remember to treat the weird ones with love and respect. Ask respectful questions and write the piece objectively. Just report. Let the readers form their own opinions.

That's class.

You get a few of these interviews under your belt and you'll be able to interview anybody.

An Ode to the Puff Job

If you're a reporter for a small-town paper, you already know what a puff job is. If not, here's a quick definition: the fastest, surest way to becoming a talented interviewer.

That's because the publisher/advertising manager of the *Valley Weekly Miracle* will tell a prospective advertiser, "And if you agree to advertise with us each week for a month, we'll have Slim write a story about you."

Oh boy ….

But if this task appeals to your journalistic masochism, you can volunteer your services for the *Valley Weekly Miracle* and have some fun. Why?

Because this is a great challenge. The greatest challenge. This is the Super Bowl and World Series of interviewing.

Your job will be to get Pete aside down at the hardware store and find something interesting about him that will not say "Go to Pete's hardware store and buy something." You need to find something interesting about Pete that probably has nothing whatever to do with hardware and make a story out of it. In short, the challenge is to write a story about Pete that no reader will think is a puff job.

The old saying is, there are no boring people, just incompetent interviewers, or that's how I see it, at any rate.

Forget the danged resume'

Well, at least don't base the interview on it. We can use it as an ice breaker.

Let's face it, if we are given 15 column inches in the paper to introduce Pete at the hardware store to our readers, and Pete is 63 years old, there isn't enough space to write about his life.

So what we have to do is look for that little part about Pete that captures our imagination and attention.

I call it "extracting the kernel." It's finding that little thing that sets Pete apart from all other hardware store owners everywhere. So how do we do it?

To begin with, Pete's going to be nervous about the

interview because he thinks you're there to write about the price of nuts and bolts and chainsaw oil, and he hopes he's up to speed on the inventory at the store. He isn't aware, nor does he even suspect, that you are there to learn about *him*.

So we can trot out the resume' questions to get the first pickle out of the jar.

To put Pete at ease with us, we show him we're interested in him. We want to know where he was born, where he went to high school, if he participated in sports there, if he was in the military, and stuff like that. Wife's name. How many kids. How long he has lived in the valley.

Pete can relax and answer these questions easily, because 1. He knows the answers, and 2. He's beginning to see that you're actually interested in him more than the price of hammers. Always remember this: the most important person in the world to Pete is Pete, just as the most important person in the world to you is you.

Listen for clues

During the resume' part of the interview, smile a lot and follow through on the answers he gives. Look for places where you can dig a little deeper into what makes Pete tick.

If Pete should say, for example, "Well, I played

basketball in high school for the first three years," what's your next question?

"So why didn't you play basketball as a senior, Pete?"

"Well, after the accident, I couldn't rebound much…"

Accident? Oh yes…

What if he answers, "I had to go to work after school to help out the family and couldn't make practice any longer."

Help out the family? Why?

Dad was killed in a plane crash? Mom died of cancer and he had to help raise the younger children? The family was suddenly homeless?

See how this works?

It's called peeling back the layers to get to the kernel of the story and makes Pete … well, Pete.

But there are always those whose uniqueness isn't readily apparent. We'll have to dig.

So how do we do that?

Here are a few questions to consider: Do you play a musical instrument? What are your hobbies? What's your favorite movie? What would you like to be doing 10 years from now? Are our children today heading in the right direction?

And to his answer to any of these questions, you can then ask why.

The why questions are your lever, your tire iron, to

peel back the layers.

Pete says, "Well, I played clarinet in junior high, but then I quit."

Why?

"Because I got really busy making things in wood shop."

What kinds of things?

"I kinda specialized in old-fashioned furniture."

How'd you become interested in that?

"Well, after our house burned down …"

That's how it's done.

Let's hear it for the What If's

When all else fails in an attempt to extract that kernel, you can always fall back on the What If's.

To illustrate, I'd like you to meet Doris:

Doris (not her real name because she's still around, even if she doesn't read) owns a handmade beauty parlor on a dirt alley. There I was, cruising around looking for someone with a pulse whom I could interview. Three hours until deadline, of course. I saw the beauty parlor sign on a tree next to a dirt alley, with an arrow pointing inland. Someone with a beauty parlor on a dirt alley? Hey, gotta be a story there.

So I drove in and met Doris.

"Hi, Doris. My name is Slim, I'll bet a lot of really funny things have happened here at your beauty parlor."

"Oh my yes!" she said, with a knee-slapping laugh.

"Mind if I interview you for the paper?"

"Oh, that would be great!"

So I called the photographer and told him how to get there and sat down with Doris.

"So Doris," I said, after we'd done the obligatory resume' stuff, "what's the funniest thing that ever happened here?"

"Well," she said, trying and failing to keep a straight face while confronting the Human Comedy, "you know I always do old Mrs. Williamson on Friday? Always on Friday? Her son brings her over and then comes to pick her up, 'cuz she's kinda old and doesn't drive any more?

"Well, one day I was just ready to finish her up. Had her hair all teased up and was ready to do the final combing, and her son drove up in front. He didn't even get out of the car. He saw his mother's hair all teased up through the window and thought she wasn't almost done, so he just drove home!"

Then I listened to raucous laughter while I told myself, "Randles, if that's the funniest thing that ever happened here, you are a dead man."

So I started digging and discovered that Doris 1. Didn't know what was going on in the world, 2. Couldn't care less, 3. Had never been married, 4. No kids. 5. Didn't really have opinions on anything in the world, and 6. Had never been more than 100 miles from the house where she was born, and which happened to be the house she still lived in.

And the photographer's on his way …

So I trotted out thewhat if's.

"So Doris, what if you could go anywhere you wanted to in the world? Where would you go?"

"Disneyland."

"Why Disneyland?"

"I want to see Mickey Mouse."

Dead man, Randles. Dead, dead….

"Now Doris, what would you do if money were no object?"

And her eyes lit up. I mean, like Hollywood grand-opening searchlights!

"You mean …?"

"Yes. If you had all the money you ever wanted and could do anything you liked with it…"

"Oh … wow! Anything?"

"Anything."

She smiled at me and whispered conspiratorially. "I'd get someone to paint my bedroom!"

Randles … you are a …

Well, no I'm not, because Doris had revealed herself

with that statement. Not everyone has dreams of Paris in April, of meeting the President, of running rafts down the Grand Canyon or becoming an astronaut.

Sometimes just getting someone to paint your bedroom is the stuff of dreams.

So I wrote it just that way. Doris's story. And while I realized that a lot of people would feel pity for her, I didn't. I found out what Doris was like and told her story. She loved it. There's a one-chair beauty parlor on a dirt alley today that has my story framed and hanging on the wall.

Thank you, Doris, for letting us get to know you.

And that's when the what if's come in handy.

Here comes Joe …

So while I'm in the storytelling mood, I want to introduce you to my pal Joe.

I was sports editor, photographer, cops reporter, feature writer, and emptied the ash trays for a weekly newspaper in a small town smack in the middle of California's farming country. The publisher came to me and told me he wanted me to do a puff piece on Joe, who was our newest advertiser. Joe, he explained, owned a small shack four miles out of town on a country road where he sold sandwiches.

So I grabbed a camera and set out to find Joe. Joe

was his real name, because if he's still alive, he'd be 110 or more and he won't care.

But at this time, our pal Joe was about 60. Real nice guy. Friendly, quiet, and deadly sincere about the interview.

In the course of two full hours of questions and answers, here's what I discovered:

Joe washed dishes in a café in a town 15 miles away for 40 years. He'd never played sports. Never had a pet. Never had a serious girlfriend. Never been in the military. Never met a celebrity. Never been hospitalized. Never been in a car wreck. Never learned to play a musical instrument. Didn't have a favorite movie. Sometimes he'd read as many as one book a year. Cookbooks. Watched television but didn't have any special programs. And when the historic highlights of the past 40 years were going on (Pearl Harbor, Hiroshima, Presidential elections and assassinations) he was washing dishes 15 miles away and was too busy to pay much attention.

If money were no object, he'd buy another table and a couple of chairs for his customers.

So what could I write about Joe?

Well, what was it that set him apart from everyone else? Just this: Nothing had ever happened to Joe. He had managed to live 60 years without anything happening to him. Things like triumph, failure, exaltation, heartbreak and compound fractures had zipped right past him and he didn't really think he'd missed that much.

So that was my story. The man nothing happened to. He loved it. It got framed and hung next to the menu board for many sandwiches to come.

And after that, Joe could claim one interesting thing: he'd had a story written about him in the local paper.

One good interviewing tip is to ask your subject if he/she has advice for young people. Often you'll be amazed by what you'll get.

I not only interviewed my good friend, Max Evans, about his illustrious career as a novelist (*The Rounders*, *Bluefeather Fellini*, *The Hi Lo Country*), but I am his biographer, and spent more than three years putting his book together. As we were wrapping it up, I asked if he had any advice for young writers. Max grinned and looked at me with his battle-scarred face and said, "Never hit a critic."

Personal story here: If you're driving down a rural road and see a sign that says "Barrel Racing Bantam Chickens for Jesus" and you don't stop the car and do a story, you're reading the wrong book. I stopped and got the story. Sometimes it isn't hard to find an interesting subject.

Interviewing celebrities

Not as easy as one might think. The trick is to learn things about these people that no one else knows. I sure didn't know this when, in the summer of 1964, I was sent to a celebrity golf tournament at Lake Tahoe to interview Joe DiMaggio. One of the nicest guys you could ever meet, and a guy who appreciated honesty.

And here was my first question:

"Nice to meet you, Joe. Now I've been a reporter for almost a week now and don't know what the hell I'm doing. What do *real* reporters ask you?"

He smiled kindly and told me. And I took notes.

But after you actually learn how to interview someone, and know what the hell you're doing, here's some tips.

Let me tell you about Senator Ernest Gruening of Alaska. When I interviewed this amazing man, he was in his late 80s, retired from politics, and was researching yet another book. When he was growing up in Boston, his father insisted he become a doctor, as Dad was a doctor, too. So young Ernest went to medical school and graduated and became a doctor. He asked his dad if he were satisfied now, and Daddy beamed and said yes, so Dr. Ernest Gruening took a job as a cub reporter on the *Boston Globe*! While ascending to the rank of managing editor of one of the nation's largest dailies in New York, Ernest managed to go through law school and write several scholarly books.

Then Franklin Roosevelt appointed him territorial governor of Alaska. Many contend he almost single-handedly pushed through statehood for Alaska, and then was elected Alaska's first United States Senator.

And there I was, sitting down with this living legend, who was a quiet, polite little old man. I got the interview, by the way, because I was pals with his grandson, Clark.

So what do you ask a man like this?

"Senator, what do you consider your greatest achievement?"

Without hesitation, he said, "I ended racial discrimination in Alaska."

He explained that when he arrived there, he discovered signs in many of the businesses saying "No Natives Allowed." The movie theaters had separate sections for Natives and whites in the audience. Natives – capital N – is the polite and socially acceptable term for Indians, Eskimos and Aleuts in Alaska.

"A territorial governor," he told me, "has terrible powers. So I started at one end of Fourth Avenue in Anchorage with a federal marshal. I went in each of the stores and restaurants and said, 'I'm Governor Gruening, and if that sign isn't down in ten minutes I'm putting a lock on your door.'"

By the time he reached the other end of the street, the word was out and the signs were down. He didn't even have to go to Fairbanks or other cities.

And no one had asked him that question before, which tickled him. He said something else, too.

"When I was first flying around, visiting the Native villages, I got to one Eskimo village on the coast and they brought out a village elder who was completely blind. I met him and looked at his eyes and could tell he had cataracts, which could be fixed. We took him with us to Anchorage and he was operated on and got his sight back."

He smiled, "And they say it doesn't pay to be a doctor, eh?"

Find a question no one else has asked. Ask it.

My interview with Louis L'Amour for *California Living* magazine illustrated this point well. He'd been a famous writer for more than 30 years, and was in fact the best-selling writer of all time. His Westerns were to be found, literally, in the bunkhouse and the White House. And he'd been interviewed by everyone and his cousin's dog over the years, too.

He was billed as "America's storyteller," so what question should I ask him? Well, I asked him what I thought was the most logical question ever: "If we were sitting around a campfire some night, what story would you tell?"

And he perked up and said, "No one's ever asked me that before."

He went on to tell me about the time he was camping out in the Takla Makan Desert in western China and hearing the camel bells of the ghost caravans on the nearby Silk Road. It was great.

But why was he surprised that I'd asked that particular question?

It was evidently the right one, because I was able to chill the blood of at least some of the readers with it. He was pleased. So was I.

So sharpen up these various arrows in your interview quiver: the what if's, the question no one asks, and especially the why questions. The why questions lead to more why questions, which is why I'm particularly fond of them. Also, the one irritating question a four-year-old asks is why.

Those four-year-olds don't have any moss growing on them, do they? Who says we can't learn from pre-schoolers?

And the result is that we often find ourselves looking at the kernel of that person. We're introducing someone to his/her neighbors. How would you do it in one sentence? How would you do it in a paragraph? How would you do it in 15 column inches? These are the questions we should ask ourselves while the interview is still going on.

What, in effect, is the essence of Pete down at the hardware store? What makes him special, different? What makes him tick? What makes him Pete?

One celebrity interview sticks in my mind, and I'd like to tell you about it. Former New Mexico Governor Garrey Carruthers seemed like a decent sort when I met him, so I asked him if – when his term ended – I could interview him about what it was like, personally, to be governor. A no-politics kind of interview. He thought it was a fine idea, and a few months later I drove up to Santa Fe for the interview.

We talked about how much time away from his family it took, and those kinds of things, and then I said, "I understand you didn't have a drink the entire time you were governor."

"No," he said. "Not the whole time."

On the Fourth of July during his first year in office, he had friends over at the mansion and was out back flipping burgers on the grill. He'd had a couple of beers and was feeling pretty mellow.

"Then the phone rang and they told me four murderers had escaped from the state pen in Santa Fe and were running around," he said. "Well, this was a big deal and I needed to do things and I wasn't razor sharp. So after that, I decided I wouldn't drink while I was governor."

And that little story told me, and my readers, quite a bit about Garrey Carruthers.

Here kernel, kernel...

So we search until we find what we think is that little kernel that tells us what this person is like. Super. So where do we use it in the story?

Well, that can vary. A lot of times, you'll want to lead with that kernel, because it tells a story, but every now and then you might want to pull an O. Henry and drop the kernel at the end of your story. It depends. And you get to decide just what "depends" means.

I'll tell you about a decision I made once, however, which might help illustrate this.

It was my interview with the *feng shui* lady. It's pronounced fung shway, by the way.

The *feng shui* lady made her living as a consultant to folks designing buildings. She explained to me how she used this ancient Chinese art of planning and design and where to put furniture to bring harmony to a home or business. I learned about not plugging up energy when it wants to flow somewhere.

I decided I had a really interesting job, meeting

people like the *feng shui* lady.

So when I wrote the piece, I explained all these things, only adding in the last sentence how her cat box sat next to her fridge in the kitchen.

See?

Sometimes the kernel is powerful ...

As it was with my (I thought) routine interview for a story on Russian Orthodox Easter eggs.

Shortly before Easter one year, I saw several beautifully decorated Easter eggs for sale at a local feed store. The proprietor said they were made by an old Russian lady who lived nearby.

Well, no they weren't. They were made by an old Ukrainian lady who lived nearby. A great many Ukrainians, it turns out, aren't partial to Russians, and she was one of them. I called and asked if I could come over and do a story on these beautiful eggs and – through her daughter, who was more fluent in English – she said to come on over.

I'm sure you've seen these eggs, or pictures of them, anyway. They are very colorful and are decorated with Christian symbols and Orthodox churches and flowers and things. They are called *pisanki*, if you're taking notes.

I went over to the house and here was a very old lady

wearing traditional Easter clothes and with a whole flock of these eggs laid out in front of her in the kitchen. Again through the translating help of her daughter – and her daughter was retired, by the way – she told me how *pisanki* were made to give to friends in the Old Country. Easter gifts. And girls would make them and give them to young fellows they were sweet on.

Then she explained (and showed me) how they were made, one color at a time, and baked in the oven and how this was a long process. I was taking notes and had enough for a how-to story on Easter *pisanki* for my readers.

Then the daughter mentioned that mother insisted on making these every Easter as a reminder.

And then I was smart enough to ask, "As a reminder of what?"

Then out came the old lady's story, as she sat there painting these eggs, patiently, one at a time.

When World War II broke out, she and her husband had a farm, had a teenage daughter (this one) and a son about eight years old. They were happy there in the rural Ukraine. Then the Russian soldiers invaded, sacked the farm and killed her husband. A short time later, here came the German soldiers, who killed most of her animals and burned down the house.

So she took the two kids, and a milk cow, and walked

across Europe!

It took a very long time to do it, but she kept on. Along the way, someone killed and ate the cow. She and the kids got to Dresden, Germany, on the very day our bombers turned the whole place into a campfire. They holed up in a movie theater which was being used as a bomb shelter. We bombed that, too, and in the process, blew the arm off her young son.

Then they started off again and finally reached the border between Soviet-held Germany and American-held Germany just as the war was ending. She said the Russian soldiers told her not to go to the American side, as the Americans would kill them on sight, but she did, anyway.

She and the two kids were welcomed by the Americans and given food and shelter in a displaced persons camp.

On Easter Sunday, 1945.

They emigrated to the United States and lived in New Jersey for many years. And the *pisanki* were to remind them of terror and pain and persistence and love.

Turned out to be quite a bit more than a how-to piece on decorating Easter eggs, didn't it?

…and sometimes the kernel is funny

Another story that started out as routine here. I was in that central California farming town, around 1968, I guess, and the boss sent me out to interview the first local kid to come home from the Vietnam War.

I went over to his house. Nice, quiet kid. I asked him about his war experiences and he said he didn't have any. But weren't you there for a whole year? Yes, but I didn't do any war stuff.

This went on for a while, and there was obviously something he didn't want to tell me. Finally, he broke down.

"Look," he said, "I didn't shoot anybody and nobody shot at me. The truth is I drove a garbage truck in Saigon."

Oh great, I thought, selfishly. And there had been times, in earlier years, where I would have thrown in the journalistic towel at this point. But I didn't.

"You mean to tell me you spent a year in a war zone and you weren't ever scared?"

"Well, just that one night was all."

Well, on that one night (I pried out of him) he was making the rounds at the Army base where he was stationed. He and the good ol' garbage truck. He stopped in front of the Bachelor Officer's Quarters, around midnight, to load their trash into the truck. A colonel was heading home at that time and got really excited.

"Son, there's a bomb in your truck!" he yelled. "I can hear it ticking!"

Other officers came pouring out of the dormitory, and – in their skivvies – were pulling garbage out of the truck as they frantically tried to find the bomb. Finally, another colonel came up and said, "Look, Son, I'm sorry, but you have to get in that truck and drive it the hell away from this building. Get it out away from things, get out, and run like crazy. And God be with you!"

So our soldier ran around and jumped in the cab and saw that he'd left his turn signal on!

Don't give up easily on what looks at first like a non-story.

For those readers who haven't been told this journalistic story (it's not true), I'll spill it for you.

A sports editor of a big paper sent a cub sports reporter out to cover a baseball game one afternoon. A few hours later, the reporter came back, sat at his desk, and began to read the funnies.

"Where's the story?" asked the editor.

"There isn't any story," the reporter answered.

"No story? Well, what happened at the game?"

"There wasn't any game."

"No game? Why not?"

He shrugged. "Stadium burned down."

Can't happen? Well, yes it can. It happened to a reporter who was covering a fishing tournament for me. When he got back after watching the best fishermen in the United States attempt to commit bass capture for two days, he told me there was no story because the fish weren't biting.

Well, I said, just give us the results and that'll have to do us.

Nobody caught any fish, he said.

Hold on ... the best fishermen in the nation spent two days pursuing fish in what is supposed to be the hottest fishing lake in the state and no one caught any fish? Not a one?

Yes.

"And that isn't a story?"

His eyes lit up at that point. The people who rented boats and tackle at that lake weren't too happy with us, but the story was good. And it went all over the country on wire service.

Keep your eyes and ears open for what is really interesting. And remember, unless it's an assignment, always query the editor first. When you get the go-ahead, you'll probably know what kinds of questions the editor wants you to ask. Sure is better to just do the interview once, isn't it?

TEN

Let's find some story ideas

We need story ideas. We need several at a time, actually, so we can query editors and get on down the road to journalistic excellence, *que no*? Que you bet!

We'll also need a blend of how-to, personality profiles, cutting edge advances in our chosen line of interest, history of various parts of our chosen line and whatever else offers itself. So how do we do this?

Methodically.

This is not just thrilling and fun, it's a business, so we have to get our fun while actually thinking and planning. I'm 71 years old and I can almost do that now.

But we should try.

We'll stick with the fish–in-a-tank theme for an example, but we should never be limited to that. And we won't be.

So let's start off finding the easy stuff.

Personality profiles

These are sellers. So what's a really easy way of

finding interesting people for a national magazine?

Read the local paper

If there's a "character" in there who still farms with horses, and the local paper does a piece on him, you might want to bounce the idea off an editor or two of a national farm magazine. Now this would only be eye-catching, however, if the guy in question isn't farming with horses for religious reasons, i.e. Amish. If he is, that would not be uncommon, and what we're looking for is offbeat.

But you read the piece the local reporter did on the guy and discover he just likes horses, or it reminds him of how he did it as a kid. So you query an editor? Nope. You go talk to this man, or call him up. Find out if he'll even talk with you about it. It would be very embarrassing to get a go-ahead from an editor and then learn that your subject wouldn't be interested in having a story written about him. So find that out first. Maybe the guy didn't like the story the local reporter did on him. Maybe his friends or family teased him about it. So find out.

"Mr. Smith? My name is Bob White, and I'm a writer. I saw that great story John Peters wrote about you in the *Valley Weekly Miracle* last Thursday, and wondered if I could interview you for a magazine article. You wouldn't mind? Hey, that's super. Let me bounce the idea off my editor and see if they'll go for it, and then I'll get back to you and we can set something up."

Not bad, huh? You already discovered, in a 30-second phone call, that 1. He liked the story in the paper, and 2. He wouldn't mind finding himself in the pages of a magazine.

Now you're free to query editors until you get a go-ahead. If you should run into a spate of we-ain't-interesteds from several editors, you can safely can this idea. But it's a really good idea to then call Mr. Smith back, let him know your editor isn't interested right now, and thank him for his patience and interest. Why? Because it's the right thing to do.

Hit the local "character" library

We've already mentioned this: bartenders, waitresses, barbers and hairdressers. And don't forget the guy at the feed store. Did you know Purina makes Monkey Chow? Yes they do. And the guy at the feed store can fill you in on any monkey lovers in town, or snake handlers, or any of the offbeat crowd.

Hit the internet

Of course. If you can't find people on there to interview, you aren't trying very hard. So how do you surf around and find someone?

Go to Google and type in things like "Goldfish swallowing," "Flat Earth Society," "UFO kidnap victims," "Horse healers," "Bloodhound trainers," "Rattlesnake recipes," "Knife throwing for fun and profit," and maybe "Grandmothers who've given birth."

There are hundreds of other things you'll be able to think of better than me. The goldfish swallowers may not fit the fish-tank magazines, but there are places for them, too.

So, for our fish-tank forum, type in things like "New ideas in fish tanks," "New cures for ick,"

"easy way to clean an aquarium." You get the idea. And what you'll get, of course, will be stories that other writers have already written and sold on the subjects, right? So what you have to do is get smart here. If a woman in Lake Champlain is interviewed by someone else about a new way to clean an aquarium, look in that story for other possibilities. Did she mention having developed the hobby in Brazil? Why Brazil? Does she sound interesting as a "character" who would make a good personality profile for another fish mag?

Each human being has several stories in them. We aren't just one-dimensional.

But, you say, that woman lives in Lake Champlain and I'm in Kansas City!

That is why God invented the telephone.

Cutting-edge stories

These will probably be confined, more than likely, to our field of interest. Fish in tanks, right?

We'll definitely want a couple of cutting-edge pieces hanging around in our query quiver and trying to find a home. So how do we find out what's new? Get a list of companies that make fish tanks, filters, pumps, even that fake seaweed stuff and call them up. Hey, what's new? What will your company have out for us next year?

You think any business can pass up an opportunity for free advertising like this? Nope.

(The fastest way to get fired or blackballed is to try to charge someone to write a piece about them. Don't ever do it.)

You can certainly get a line-up of these businesses by going on the internet. We're using pet fish as an example, of course, but it's no different with cooking, horses, construction, guns, boating, dog training, television or just about anything. Just go try it. For laughs, type in "aquarium supplies" and see what happens.

I just did. Five million, eight hundred thousand

entries. Told you so.

And magazines love cutting-edge stories.

Go to the zoo

Our zoo has an aquarium. Maybe yours does, too. Go there, talk to the people who care for the fish. Sound them out. What's the biggest problem with taking care of the fish? How do they know which fish are compatible in the same tank and which will eat all the others? What's new in fish food? How do you clean one of those huge tanks when it has a hammerhead shark in it?

And of course, if fish tanks aren't your passion, go talk to people who are involved with your interest, whatever it may be.

History

History is something that appeals to almost every reader. I'm not just thinking of Paul Revere, or that kind of history. Although, if your magazine passion is horses, what kind of horse did Paul ride? What kind of saddle? Bridle? Bit? How was the horse shod?

But the history of our fish-tank passion has very interesting possibilities, too. What was the earliest mention of keeping fish in captivity? What kind of fish were the first to be penned up? Why? Who made the first modern glass-sided fish tank? Who solved the aeration problem in supplying oxygen to the water?

Are there any manmade fish? (Hey, this is not a goofy question. The mule is a manmade animal. The modern turkey is a manmade animal who cannot survive without people. So is the Holstein milk cow which can't live without us.).

I don't know if there are manmade fish, but it is a reasonable question to ask.

Is anyone trying to create a manmade fish through cloning? You know … Super Salmon? That would make a good cutting-edge story.

Look into your passion's past and learn about the pioneers in that field. How did certain practices in that field come about? Who did them? Why did they think it necessary?

I truly believe most writers could earn a decent living if all they ever wrote about was the history of their field, and the personality profiles. These are heavy-duty sought-after stories by editors.

How-to stories

There probably aren't as large a range of stories from a how-to perspective as some of the other areas, but there are quite a few. And magazines suck them up like chocolate ice cream. Just look at the covers of most magazines at the supermarket. How to 1. Make your lover ecstatic, 2. Create a monstrous income for retirement, 3. Teach your dog quantum physics, etc.

In our fish-tank world, we could go to the pet store and ask who is an avid local fish tanker and see what they can teach us. Usually, good questions to ask a long-time aquari-nut would be "What's the biggest mistake first-time fish keepers make?" "What's the best way to raise baby fish?" "How do you repair an aquarium?"

Worth a query letter or two. And, as is usually the case, an hour spent with a dyed-in-the-wool fish fanatic will lead to a dozen story ideas to salt away for the future.

ELEVEN

Should I query on a book, too?

You bet. In almost every case. You can find out for sure by referring to Writer's Market. Little tip here; if a book publisher wants a completed non-fiction book without a query first, take a really close look at this company. Look up the books they've published before. You might even want to call the editor. Why?

A book is a whole lot of work. A lot of work. It's a lot of work for you to write it and it's a lot of work for them to read it. At best, a book is a magazine article on steroids. So consider carefully before going to all that work, slapping on all those stamps and then facing the possibility of the whole thing being returned six months later.

Novels

It's different with fiction. With a novel, almost all publishers will want to see a completed manuscript. It stands to reason. With a novel, you're leaning almost entirely on the writer's skills (soul soaring, etc.) and not as much on the subject.

How far do you think Steinbeck would've gotten with *East of Eden* by querying first.

"A teenage boy in Salinas doesn't get along with his folks."

Yeah.

I just happen to be one of those rare people who did sell a novel through a query letter, detailed outline and sample chapters. I didn't even think it was possible until they asked me to send them those things. I did. They sent me an advance check for $5,000! They ended up not publishing the novel because the particular imprint label (this was one of the largest publishing houses in the world) went belly up. So they wished me luck and told me to keep the money. That was really good, because it was already spent! That novel was eventually published by one of the smallest (and best) publishing companies in the world. They did a great job on it. This publishing company is two women in a ghost town in Alaska. They publish one book a year. (They've published two of mine now, which is a real honor.)

The only … *only* reason the large publishing house would consider sending me money for a novel they haven't read yet is very simple. The editor there knew my work and was a fan of mine. I'm sure Tom Clancy could get an advance from them, too. They know his work, too.

I'm an established writer these days, with a good reputation, and I still am expected to submit a whole novel first. It's only right. It's something of a bother, it costs postage money and there's a lot of waiting. And no, don't ever submit it to more than one publishing house at a time.

Non-fiction books

Now let's look at non-fiction books, because they are immensely more important in the publishing world than novels. We'll get into writing that fiction soul-soaring stuff after a while. It's fun.

But let's look at writing a book, for money, by approaching editors by query letter.

A book is a big project. They come in all sizes and thicknesses, of course, and you can go through *Writer's Market* to jot down a half-dozen publishers who might be interested in the subject of your book. They'll tell you the range of length to stay within if you're considering them.

Because a book is a big deal, most publishers want, in addition to a (somewhat longer) query letter, a detailed outline of the book and a couple of sample chapters. They don't say this, but I will … make one of those chapters your first chapter. They'll want to see how well you can capture the reader's attention, for one, and then the first chapter in a non-fiction book also usually lays out what the reader can expect to find in the rest of the book. If the reader is going to like you, it will happen in the first chapter.

Two chapters should be enough: Chapter One, and another that you're particularly proud of. The other chapter, in my opinion, should really have some meat in it. It should tell the reader stuff that was the reader's reason for buying the book in the first place. Of course, if you read in *Writer's Market* that the publisher wants to read three chapters, or four, give them to him. These are just things I've learned from my experiences and should be taken as suggestions.

What should we put in that query letter?

A book query varies from a magazine query in several ways. The main thing I'd put in the letter is a reason to publish this particular book. Why did you write it? You have something to communicate, right? To whom? Why? You'll need to answer those questions in the letter to give the editor a reason why he should consider going to all the trouble of sending it first to a reader and paying that reader a couple of hundred dollars to see whether the book should be published or used as a door stop. Then, if it gets by the reader, to sit down and read it himself before deciding whether or not to submit it to the committee.

Oh yes, there's a committee. These are business people. With a magazine piece, you're generally dealing with one person. That person has the horses to decide what to put in the magazine and what to leave out. If he chooses unwisely, the higher ups will raise eyebrows. If he chooses unwisely too often, he'll be looking for work.

But with a book, there are more considerations. We're talking about a long turnaround time here, usually about a year, between the time the book is accepted and when you'll get your ten copies in the mail.

Publishing a book takes months and costs thousands of dollars. A book goes through any number of people before it hits the book stores. The publisher will have a copy editor go over it for mistakes of either a factual or grammatical nature. Then there's the publicity department, working hand in hand with the sales department. Depending on the size and heft of the company doing the publishing, this could vary from days and weeks of work and thousands of dollars, to doing nothing at all.

Then there's the art department, hashing over ideas for the cover design.

All these things take time and money. And you caused it!

But there's a bottom line here on any book, fiction or non-fiction. The publisher has only one question:

How many of these things can we sell?

That's it. If you can give him a book he can sell, you'll probably get another chance later on, too.

So in a query letter, let's give the editor an idea of how many people there are out there who want this information. Potential buyers. Let's look at another silly sample query letter, but this time for a book.

Sample Book Query Letter

Douglas Madness
Propinquity Press
New York, NY

Dear Sir:

Each year, more than two million families in the United States buy goldfish for their homes, a hobby which science has proven helps people relax, gives them a worthwhile hobby, and even lowers blood pressure in the elderly.

Despite that, few goldfish owners understand the basics of goldfish husbandry, causing more than 1.5 million fish annually to end their careers with a quiet flush.

My proposed book, "Keeping Goldfish Healthy and Happy," will be a simple, straightforward and fun guide to assuring success in keeping these pets.

Enclosed please find two sample chapters from the proposed book, and a detailed outline of the contents. If you are interested in looking at the completed manuscript, I can have that to you in six months.

Thank you for your time,

Mickey Finn
1234 Glass Bowl Ave.
Flushing, NY
(212) 843-6789

Now that's a fairly straightforward query letter, just like the one we used for the magazine article, but this time we sleuthed around and discovered how many potential readers there are for this book. If Mickey Finn has an extensive background in goldfish husbandry, I would add that. But I'm assuming he isn't a world-renowned expert on fish. In that case, all we really need to know is if Mickey can deliver a good book on the care of goldfish. You might want to know why Mickey left so much time to get the manuscript turned in. I would too. A book on the care of goldfish will probably not be very big … maybe one of those little books you find on a rack at the pet store, alongside books on paper training chuckawallas and exercising the cat.

Well, if Mickey can get a go-ahead on looking at a book on goldfish, he can probably turn it in in a month or two and be considered a whiz bang. Better that than to say he'll have it in a month and then blow the deadline, right?

One of the things editors really do understand is that, with a professional writer like Mickey, the goldfish book is probably only one of several ongoing projects Mickey's working on, and will therefore need more time than if this were his only project.

But what if this is Mickey's only writing project and he waits tables for a living? No one else has to know that, do they?

Some publishers want to see a resume' or at least a synopsis of a resume' if the book being written requires expertise from the writer. This is especially true with a how-to book.

Another example…

Here's an actual query letter draft for a how-to book I wrote.

Editor

Book publisher
City

Dear

After more than 30 years as journalist and hunting guide, I strongly subscribe to the old saying, "I'd rather be lucky than good," but there are ways hunters can swing the odds heavily in their favor when it comes to elk.

"Dancing Through Dark Timber, a commonsense approach to elk hunting" takes a practical-yet-fun approach to hunting one of the nation's most popular species, and in at least one case, smashes ages-old "We've always done it this way" thinking. I see this book as becoming a back-pocket guide hunters can refer to when in the woods.

Enclosed please find two sample chapters, along with a detailed outline and a resume'.

Please let me know if you'd like to see the book.

Thanks for your time,

Slim Randles

By the way, the book is now called *The Backpocket*

Guide to Hunting Elk, from Wee Orp Books. Buy a bunch, I need the money!

Anyway, you'll notice that I did not, in this case, put how many hunters there are in the United States (20 million, by the way) as I'd advised doing earlier. Why not? Because this particular kind of book would only be published by an outdoor publishing house, and they already know how many hunters there are.

If you're writing a cookbook, you probably wouldn't have to tell the publisher how many people eat every day, either. But, if three million people really enjoy Cajun food, and you've written a Cajun recipe book, I'd sure throw that in.

In the elk hunting book query, I did refer to smashing "We've always done it this way" thinking.

That's a teaser. Oh, it's in there, all right. I have some very definite ideas, you see, on the proper care of game meat in the field and they do fly in the face of tradition. But now the publisher (who is in the same field) will have to ask to see the book to find out what my oddball ideas are.

If I were to write a book on how to pack the backyard horse to go have some fun in the mountains (I packed mules for several years), I would do my homework and find how many backyard horses there are in the U.S. (more than at any time in history), the ages of a majority of horse owners (fact: most American horses are owned by teenage girls), and how many pack saddles are sold each year. There are only a couple of companies who make these, so that shouldn't be hard to nail down. I would then put that info in a query letter, because even a horse book publisher might not have any experience with packing. It's not that common with most horsemen.

How about that outline thing?

Ah yes, the outline! Hey, you were in fourth grade once, right? You remember how to outline. Basically, just list the ingredients in each one. Most publishers want a detailed outline, so we need to be a bit more specific.

Let's outline a chapter on a book you're familiar with … this one!

Chapter One
Hey, anyone can be a writer!

Well, no they can't and yes they can. Not everyone has the ability to communicate well.

An example is given of a "leg man" for a newspaper who had to call in to a rewrite man because he did a great job of reporting, but couldn't write the story.

Yes they can because a publisher doesn't care what color you are, what religion you are, how old you are, how inexperienced you are.

There are three vital ingredients a writer must have: talent, a love of the language and an insatiable curiosity.

All writing is reporting. Examples are given showing how even fiction, songwriting and poetry are still reporting.

Chapter Two
Today's magazine market

And so on ….

It's not difficult to write an outline, but it is time-consuming and always drives me nuts.

Is there any other reason to outline the book?

You betcha. You'll want to outline the book before you even write your sample chapters, before you send off a query letter. You'll want to outline your book so your mind will sort things out before you write.

A book's a big project. What I usually do (and I'm sure many writers do it differently) is to jot down first the main ingredients in the book. These are the things I want to explain, include, etc.

Then I'll look at the list and put them in the order I think they should be in the book. When I seem to be fairly satisfied with the order of things, I'll start adding (as I think of them) little sub ideas under each of the ingredients. In the first chapter of this book, I put in that story about the "leg man" to illustrate my point. That's the sort of thing I'll do all through outlining the book.

When my mind seems to have a handle on what I want to say – and sometimes this outlining process takes quite a while – I'll sit down and start writing. I know writers who adhere strictly to their outlines. They'll tell me how frustrating it is sometimes because they'll get to a certain point and feel like adding something, but the outline won't let them.

Hey, who's the boss here?! Who's doing the driving? This is *your* book. If you want to add something, add it. If, when all is done, it doesn't seem to work, delete it.

I find having an outline really helps me get my mind into some semblance of order and reason. After outlining a book, I feel better. I put down on paper a beginning, a middle and an end. And this works for novels as well as a how-to book on hunting elk. But don't let that outline enslave you. You wrote it, you can change it. A lot of times you'll think of something that should go in there, so put it there. You're the boss.

What I do – what works for my own disorganized mind – is to disregard the outline once I've written it. I'll stick it in the corner and forget it. Then I start writing. I know where I want to start, generally, because I've outlined it, and now I'll just concentrate on writing good stuff.

Sometimes I forget where I should go next, and I can take a look at the outline and get back on track, but I'm never going to be a slave to it. That doesn't sound like fun. I like fun.

Especially with novels

Novels can really be an adventure. Go ahead and outline it, the same as you would non-fiction, then sit down and see what happens. Why do I say that? Because that's been my experience.

I outlined my first novel *The Long Dark* and then wrote it. *The Long Dark* (the publisher named it) is a story about village life in Alaska in winter. Then I put the outline aside and sat down at the typewriter (oh yes, we used the old iron mistresses once upon a time). My characters did whatever they thought they should, I discovered, to my delight, and each day I couldn't wait to get out there and see what they were going to do.

Writing a novel has a way of taking you away from

what's going on in real life. Example:

I wrote that novel in southern California sitting outside next to a swimming pool while wearing swim trunks. See? And I was writing about blizzards and sled dogs.

And even though the story was moving around and doing little things each day that I didn't expect, it was still staying within the bounds of my basic idea for the book and heading for the conclusion I had conceived. This happened because I had outlined it first. That outline was filed 'way back deep in my mind somewhere, but it was there enough to allow me to have fun, and keep me on the main road, or close to it.

A writer's rules of thumb on a novel include 1. Never stray too far from the plot, and 2. Don't stray too often.

Outlines should never rule our lives, but they are a useful tool.

How about timing these queries?

Good question. With magazine articles, I suggested giving the editor two weeks to get back to you before flogging the story idea to someone else. With a book, I'd give the editor at least a month. Then, if you haven't heard from him, maybe send him a note asking if he'd received the query yet.

More and more publishers are sending little notes

to the writers immediately saying, "Your query has been received. Thanks for thinking of us, and you'll be hearing from us shortly."

That's awfully nice. It sure didn't used to be that way. Publishers pictured themselves floating on a cloud having coffee with Jesus, and writers were peons to be used or discarded on a whim.

Am I exaggerating? Sure. It's more fun. But there *was* an attitude.

In all these dealings with publishers and editors, you can't go wrong following the Golden Rule. A little courtesy and kindness goes a long way.

TWELVE

Okay ... let your soul soar!

Remember we talked about how no one can teach you to write? Well, that's true enough, but there are ways to help others with this magical thing called good writing. I learned this in the only journalism class I was ever in ... and I was the teacher! Yep, the University of New Mexico hired me to teach the magazine writing class back in the 1980s, and I did that for eight years. I can't be sure, but I think I was the only professor in that department who had only an honorary high school diploma and received it at age 37.

(I guarantee I learned more than anyone else ever did in that class)

But I was able to thrash around and come up with some helpful stuff for them. One of those things was on what we could have called "Soul Soaring Night." But we didn't call it anything, actually.

What I did that night was to tell the class to get as crazy and creative as they could, and then write a paragraph, there in class, on a certain subject. I remember "coffee" was one, and "music" was another one. It could have been anything.

Then I had them turn the paper face down, and I read them excerpts from what I considered great writing. At the end of that time, they were to write another paragraph on the same subject, but this time cutting loose all inhibitions.

The results were startling to me, and to them. It was hard to believe the same two paragraphs came from the same person. Why? Because the first one was tied down by convention. Our collars were still buttoned up. We were all in our places with sunshiny faces. We wrote that first paragraph telling people what we thought they expected to hear about coffee.

A typical coffee Paragraph One would go something like this:

"There's nothing like a good cup of coffee in the morning. It clears away the cobwebs of sleep and gets us started on a new day."

Then, after listening to me read some excerpts, Paragraph Two sounded more like this:

"Just let it hit the back of my throat and my starter button and shoot me out the door. Go coffee, you wonderful brew that makes life possible...."

And they would each read number one and number two out loud and you could see the light bulbs come on all over the room. Now I'm not sure we can duplicate that by writing this chapter, but we can at least give some examples and it may inspire you to cut loose.

"Cutting loose" is really a good way of putting it, because we've always been taught to color inside the lines, haven't we? We are to write calmly and logically our ideas to impart. But cutting loose (letting that soul soar) has its place, too. Stream of consciousness writing is pretty boring, because the writer may know what he's trying to say, but I usually don't. So what we're after here is something between the two extremes: boring prose on one hand and nonsensical gibberish on the other. My suggestion:

Draft your story in a semi-state of gibberish and then go back and soberly tone it down to the point where it makes sense, but doesn't kill the rhythm or the music.

I believe it was Ernest Hemingway who said a person should write drunk then edit sober, or vice versa. There's some truth in that, but you don't have to drink like Hemingway (few of us can) to get it done. You can put yourself in a semi-wild mood for that first draft, then come back in the morning, after the coffee has hit your starter button, and make sure someone else can see your point.

Make it sing!

I'll give you some examples of what I think is really good writing. To me, good writing should be like music. Music is the international language, isn't it? It touches us all. What does it have?

Rhythm. High notes. Low notes. Soft soothing passages. Bright, smashing chords. A mixture. A blending of beauty, excitement, tranquility. We should take our reader through a symphony of words, in my opinion. We want them to know this, and this, and this. And we want them to end up here. And along that route, we want them to see what we saw, to feel what we felt, and to perhaps see things the way we did.

And we want to do this with both fiction and non-fiction, and we want to do it without telling them what we think or feel, because that should be left to them.

A symphony of words? Well, why not?

Especially with a novel, you are leading the reader through a long story, aren't you? Is there any reason to bore him to death along the way? I think not!

So keep him turning pages, and turning them not just because the story line is gripping, but because you also tell it in a symphonic manner.

You can simply soothe him along smoothly for a long, lustrous time, and then slap him bang in the head.

See?

Don't be … predictable, I guess. This separates the real writers from the plodders.

So now let's have some fun and read some good stuff.

A writer could simply say that a drought came upon the land and people had a hard time getting along, but here's how a schoolmaster from South Africa put it. His name is Alan Paton and this is his opening to *Cry the Beloved Country*. Hear the haunting rhythms of Africa.

There is a lovely road that runs from Ixopo into the hills. These hills are grass-covered and rolling, and they are lovely beyond any singing of it. The road climbs seven miles into them, to Carisbrooke; and from there, if there is no mist, you look down on one of the fairest valleys of Africa. About you there is grass and bracken and you may hear the forlorn crying of the titihoya, one of the birds of the veld. Below you is the valley of the Umzimkulu, on its journey from the Drakensberg to the sea; and beyond and behind the river, great hill after great hill; and beyond and behind them, the mountains of Ingeli and East Griqualand.

The grass is rich and matted, you cannot see the soil. It

holds the rain and the mist, and they seep into the ground, feeding the streams in every kloof. It is well-tended, and not too many cattle feed upon it; not too many fires burn it, laying bare the soil. Stand unshod upon it, for the ground is holy, being even as it came from the Creator. Keep it, guard it, care for it, for it keeps men, guards men, cares for men. Destroy it and man is destroyed.

Where you stand the grass is rich and matted, you cannot see the soil. But the rich green hills break down. They fall to the valley below, and falling, change their nature. For they grow red and bare: they cannot hold the rain and mist, and the streams are dry in the kloofs.

Too many cattle feed upon the grass, and too many fires have burned it. Stand shod upon it, for it is coarse and sharp, and the stones cut under the feet. It is not kept, or guarded or cared for, it no longer keeps men, guards men, cares for men. The titihoya does not cry here any more....

Ernest Hemingway wrote a passage in *The Snows of Kilimanjaro* which bears repeating. It is the thoughts of a dying man, looking back on the things he never wrote, with regret.

No, he had never written about Paris. Not the Paris that he cares about. But what about the rest that he had never written?

*What about the ranch and the silvered gray of the sage
brush, the quick, clear water in the irrigation ditches, and
the heavy green of the alfalfa. The trail went up into the
hills and the cattle in the summer were shy as deer. The
bawling and the steady noise and slow moving mass
raising a dust as you brought them down in the fall. And
behind the mountains, the clear sharpness of the peak in
the evening light and, riding down along the trail in the
moonlight, bright across the valley. Now he remembered
coming down through the timber in the dark holding the
horse's tail when you could not see and all the stories that
he meant to write.*

*About the half-wit chore boy who was left at the ranch
that time and told not to let any one get any hay, and that
old bastard from the Forks who had beaten the boy when
he had worked for him stopping to get some feed. The
boy refusing and the old man saying he would beat him
again. The boy got the rifle from the kitchen and shot him
when he tried to come into the barn and when they came
back to the ranch he'd been dead a week, frozen in the
corral and the dogs had eaten part of him. But what was
left you packed on a sled wrapped in a blanket and roped
on and you got the boy to help you haul it, and the two
of you took it out over the road on skis, and sixty miles
down to town to turn the boy over. He having no idea*

109

that he would be arrested. Thinking he had done his duty and that you were his friend and he would be rewarded. He'd helped to haul the old man in so everybody could know how bad the old man had been and how he'd tried to steal some feed that didn't belong to him, and when the sheriff put the handcuffs on the boy he couldn't believe it. Then he'd started to cry. That was one story he had saved to write. He knew at least twenty good stories from out there and he had never written one. Why?

That is very close to stream of consciousness, and is done extremely well.

One of my favorite writers, Baker Morrow, has the soul of a poet, and when he describes a place, you're there. You not only see what's there, but you see it through the eyes of a poet, a musician. You smell it. My favorite book of his is *A Tropical Place Like That*, a collection of short stories about southern Mexico. Here's one reason why:

The source of the spring was in front of him. The water flowed up strong and cold from beneath a heavy basalt lip and the local people in ancient times had contained it in a square pool also lined by slabs of basalt and the old cypresses grew along its banks and shaded everything.

Along two edges where the shade was best, twenty or thirty women in green and purple cotton skirts and white blouses were bent down on their knees washing out their laundry. They slapped the clothes down wet against the rocks and then kneaded them like cornmeal masa and rinsed them in the chilly flowing water. Some of the women had round red osier baskets full of dirty clumps of laundry and others pulled shirts and pants and socks out of thick yellow straw baskets that had two handles each.

Behind them the clean clothes were draped out in the bright sunlight on the lush undergrowth ringing the pool. The place smelled very fresh.

Hear the rhythm? This is music, with no instruments, just the voice of the words on paper.

Here's more music:

Through the fence, between the curling flower spaces, I could see them hitting. They were coming toward where the flag was and I went along the fence. Luster was hunting in the grass by the flower tree. They took the flag out, and they were hitting. Then they put the flag back and they went to the table, and he hit and the other hit. Then they went on, and I went along the fence. Luster came away from the flower tree and we went along the fence and they stopped and we stopped and I looked through the fence while Luster was hunting in the grass.

Those are the opening lines of *The Sound and the Fury* by William Faulkner. He's not the easiest writer to read, but it's worth the effort. Faulkner, above, was writing about a game of golf as seen through the eyes of a retarded man. There is a genius in the rhythm and the innocence of the words.

Writing through the eyes of an illiterate country youth around the time of the Civil War, Mark Twain lets us see what goes through the fertile minds of boys. This is from *Huckleberry Finn*, in my opinion one of the greatest of American novels.

Making them pens was a distressed tough job, and so was the saw, and Jim allowed the inscription was going to be the toughest of all. That's the one which the prisoner has to scrabble on the wall. But he had to have it. Tom said he'd got to. There warn't no case of a state prisoner not scrabbling his inscription to leave behind, and his coat of arms.

"Look at Lady Jane Grey," he says. "Look at Gilford Dudley; look at old Northumberland! Why, Huck, s'pose it is considerable trouble? What you going to do? How you going to get around it? Jim's got to do his inscription and coat of arms. They all do."

Jim says, "Why, Mars Tom, I hain't got no coat o' arm; I hain't got nuff'n but dish yer ole shirt, en you knows I got to keep de journal on dat."

"Oh, you don't understand, Jim; a coat of arms is very different."

"Well," I says, "Jim's right, anyway, when he says he hain't got no coat of arms, because he hain't."

"I reckon I knowed that," Tom says. "But you bet he'll have one before he goes out of this – because he's going out right, and there ain't going to be no flaws in his record."

So whilst me and Jim filed away at the pens on a brickbat apiece, Jim a-making his'n out of the brass and I making mine out of the spoon, Tom set to work to think out the coat of arms. By and by he said he'd struck so many good ones he didn't hardly know which to take, but there was one which he reckoned he'd decide on.

He says, "On the scutcheon we'll have a bend or in the dexter base, a saltire murrey in the fess, with a dog, couchant, for common charge, and under his foot a chain embattled, for slavery, with a chevron vert in a chief engrailed, and three invected lines on a field azure, with the nombril points rampant on a dancette indented; crest, a runaway nigger, sable, with his bundle over his shoulder on a bar sinister; and a couple of gules for supporters, which is you and me; motto, Maggiore fretta, minore atto. Got it out of a book – means the more haste *the less speed."*

"Geewhillikins!" I says. "But what does the rest mean?"

"We ain't got no time to bother over that," he says.

"Well, anyway," I says, "What's some of it? What's a fess?"

"A fess – a fess is – you don't need to know what a fess is. I'll show him how to make it when he gets to it."

"Shucks, Tom," I says. "I think you might tell a person. What's a bar sinister?"

"Oh, I don't know. But he's got to have it. All the nobility does, and he's got to."

That was just his way. If it didn't suit him to explain a thing to you, he wouldn't do it. You might pump at him a week, it wouldn't make no difference.

Blending love, deadly serious talk about freeing a slave, braggadocio and knee-slapping humor on one page is genius.

When it comes to pure terror, it's hard to beat Edgar Allan Poe. Here is how he opened *The Telltale Heart* back in 1843:

TRUE! --nervous --very, very dreadfully nervous I had been and am; but why will you say that I am mad? The disease had sharpened my senses --not destroyed --not dulled them. Above all was the sense of hearing acute. I

114

heard all things in the heaven and in the earth. I heard many things in hell. How, then, am I mad? Hearken! and observe how healthily --how calmly I can tell you the whole story.

It is impossible to say how first the idea entered my brain; but once conceived, it haunted me day and night. Object there was none. Passion there was none. I loved the old man. He had never wronged me. He had never given me insult. For his gold I had no desire. I think it was his eye! yes, it was this! He had the eye of a vulture --a pale blue eye, with a film over it. Whenever it fell upon me, my blood ran cold; and so by degrees --very gradually --I made up my mind to take the life of the old man, and thus rid myself of the eye forever.

How should we describe a character? Height? Weight? Eye color? There are other ways, too, and what we're striving for is to find a way that is uniquely our own. Here's one way Willa Cather did it, tying it to the seasons of the year, from her book, *Lucy Gayheart.*

In Haverford on the Platte the townspeople still talk of Lucy Gayheart. They do not talk of her a great deal, to be sure; life goes on and we live in the present. But when they do mention her name it is with a gentle glow in the face or the voice, a confidential glance which says: "Yes, you, too, remember?" They still see her as a slight figure always in motion; dancing or skating, or walking swiftly with intense direction, like a bird flying home.

When there is a heavy snowfall, the older people look out of their windows and remember how Lucy used to come darting through just such storms, her muff against her cheek, not shrinking, but giving her body to the wind as if she were catching step with it. And in the heat of summer she came just as swiftly down the long shaded sidewalks and across the open squares blistering in the sun. In the breathless glare of August noons, when the horses hung their heads and the workmen "took it slow," she never took it slow. Cold, she used to say, made her feel more alive; heat must have had the same effect.

We can try to do the same thing in describing a place. Here is one that really sticks in the mind: John Steinbeck's opening paragraph in *Cannery Row*.

Cannery Row in Monterey in California is a poem, a stink, a grating noise, a quality of light, a tone, a habit, a nostalgia, a dream. Cannery Row is the gathered and scattered, tin and iron and rust and splintered wood, chipped pavement and weedy lots and junk heaps, sardine canneries of corrugated iron, honky tonks, restaurants and whore houses, and little crowded groceries, and laboratories and flophouses. Its inhabitants are, as the man once said, "whores, pimps, gamblers, and sons of bitches," by which he meant Everybody. Had the man looked through another peephole he might have said, "Saints and angels and martyrs and holy men," and he would have meant the same thing.

That's one way to encapsulate, in a few gorgeous words, the kernel of truth, the essence of a place. Here's another way, with a different culture, done by Columbian novelist Gabriel Garcia Marquez, in his opening lines of *One Hundred Years of Solitude*. Listen to the music and the flavor.

Many years later, as he faced the firing squad, Colonel Aureliano Buendia was to remember that distant afternoon when his father took him to discover ice. At that time, Macondo was a village of twenty adobe houses, built on the bank of a river of clear water that ran along a bed of polish stones, which were white and enormous, like prehistoric eggs. The world was so recent that many things lacked names, and in order to indicate them it was necessary to point. Every year during the month of March a family of ragged gypsies would set up their tents near the village, and with a great uproar of pipes and kettledrums they would display new inventions. First they brought the magnet. A heavy gypsy with an untamed beard and sparrow hands, who introduced himself as Melquiades, put on a bold public demonstration of what he himself called the eighth wonder of the learned alchemists of Macedonia. He went from house to house dragging two metal ingots and everybody was amazed to see pots, pans, tongs, and braziers tumble down from their places and beams creak from the desperation of nails and screws trying to emerge, and even objects that had been lost for a long time appeared from where they had been searched for most and went dragging along in turbulent confusion behind Melquiades' magical irons. "Things have a life of their own," the gypsy proclaimed with a harsh accent. "It's simply a matter of waking up their souls."

In my opinion, one of the greatest writers in the English language is a former cowboy from New Mexico, Max Evans. As is common with hardheaded cowboys, he learned everything in life the hard way, and writing was no exception. He taught himself. He considers his novel, *Bluefeather Fellini*, to be his masterpiece, although he's best known for the rollicking comedy, *The Rounders*. To prove that even cowboys can eventually "get it," here are the opening lines from *Bluefeather Fellini*.

It was the time of youthful jubilation, and Bluefeather Fellini – the chosen one – knew that never, never, never before had anyone his age been so blessed. In just a few days, they would be rich – rich as bankers, rich as doctors, rich as movie stars, rich as kings. Grinder the Gringo was giving him this wondrous opportunity, and if he lived a thousand years, he could never show his ample appreciation for the golden opportunity afforded him by this generous genius sitting with him in the woods at this moment.

He sat across the campfire in Twinning Canyon north of Taos, New Mexico, watching the toothless old prospector, Sam Grinder, with respect. He could hear the voices of the night birds in the forest as clearly as violins, and feel the very earth vibrate with other more muted sounds of walking and flying life. The campfire flickered on the rump of the burro feeding contentedly from a feedbag and swatting, from habit, an imaginary fly with his tail.

Now that they had eaten, Grinder took off his hat, pushed at his gray, stringy hair and took a large chew of tobacco from a paper container. He chewed with long-suffering gums until the tobacco was soft and ready for spitting. He turned his head and exuded a stream into an empty coffee can.

Bluefeather thought, "What a gentleman." All the prospectors and hunters he had known before spat into the fire to test their accuracy and enjoy the little explosions from the moisture. Grinder looked up at him, somehow knowing the young man's thoughts were too complimentary.

Also from *Bluefeather*, Max writes of war, a war he was in. It is some of the best writing I've ever seen on war, and bears including here because Evans finds a new way to tell an old story.

On the beach were parts of men, and in the water were parts of men. A small percentage were whole, however, having drowned as their landing craft disgorged them in water too deep for solid footing. The beach was a cauldron of chaos beyond the limbs and bones and scraps of torn flesh mingled with discarded gas masks, useless punctured canteens, broken and bent concrete and steel beach obstacles, erratic piles of smashed and destroyed equipment, and disabled and destroyed vehicles already being reclaimed by the sand and sea. Destruction incarnate.

Many of the seventy-two known elements of the earth, which were of such beauty and sparkle in their natural veined and disseminated forms, were here fused, amalgamated and alloyed into terribly efficient instruments of death. The same elements whose seeking and finding was Bluefeather Fellini's life's work were now particles of booming savagery just before the stillness of death. His sought-after beauty was trying to kill him, but of this he was mercifully oblivious. Violence – violated violence. Piercing, screaming steel, twanging off hard objects and thudding, slicing, piercing softer things, and on impact, blood flying into the convulsed air and becoming a red mist before running in rivulets, sinking into the wet sand searching for the birthing sea. This was the ultimate exploitation of the human wholeness – its severance. The bodies floated facedown calmly now in the sea, moving only as the mother ocean did. On land, the living crawled through the motionless dead and paused over and over next to the nonmovement to gather a bit of sulfurous air into their heaving lungs, and another tad of courage. Then forward again. Again. Again.

Bluefeather saw a lot of this, as they moved out of the water into all the above – up little canyons, in the cliffs with sniper fire and artillery harassing them almost every step. Every few yards this harassment also killed someone. But the stench of his own vomit and the excrement and urine in his olive-greens helped disguise that of exploded entrails and the vast nauseating blood-smell strong as a thousand slaughterhouses.

The war was a blur. Like a barroom brawl. There were no great organized plans and brilliant military tactics, no inflamed thoughts of glory and winning of great battles, no patriotic images of heroics and the flags of one's country waving in victory. There was simply a moving blur of frazzled images in a twenty-yard circle. This war, the world, everything, was all in this very small twenty-yard circle. That's all he knew. All he felt. All he realized of existence and nonexistence. All.

So how do you introduce a man like Max Evans to strangers? Here is how I did it for his biography, *Ol' Max Evans, the First Thousand Years.*

"Fun!" said Coyote, grinning. "That's it. That's it and all of it. You need more fun, sobersides."

"That's fine for you, Coyote," said Raven. "You roam around the country with that grin, always with that grin. You eat whatever comes along, and at night … at night you keep everyone awake with that singing of yours."

And that Raven, he shook his head all solemn-like. "Some of us have to work hard to eat."

"Ah, work!" said Coyote, closing his left eye and hopping to the left, just as an experiment. "Work is good, Raven. Sometimes even the singing is work, you know. The singing, the rapturous singing about the world. The

telling of a thousand stories. Watching the world move about you, Raven. That can be work, too."

"That's ridiculous," said Raven.

"Of course it is," said Coyote. "Ridiculous and fun. But only the best lives are ridiculous and fun. You just take my brother, for example. For him, life has been both ridiculous and fun, and that's why people can't really figure him out."

"Your brother?"

Coyote lolled his tongue out in ecstasy as he rolled over and scratched behind his ear. His eyes squinted to a close as he contemplated for just a second the parameters of sanity and the direct benefits of peak rabbit years. Then he powdered his head with dust in a coyote dance and sat spraddle-legged and grinning at the regally wise bird.

"My brother," Coyote said. "Yes, my brother has made a life of ridiculous fun an art form. He howls at the moon in the books he writes. He lives a ridiculously fun life and spits in the eye of convention."

"Your brother?"

"Has been for years now," said Coyote. "A brother in every sense. He can laugh. He can howl. He can bite and scratch. He can stare at the moon and see wondrous magic."

Then that Coyote, he laughs to see Raven shaking his head.

"Scoff if you will, Raven, but I'll tell you about my brother, anyway, because it makes a great song. A great evening song. And it's worth it.

"To start with, they call him Ol' Max ..."

This is from my novel *Sun Dog Days*. It's about a transition back to a former life.

Smokey recovered in about four days, but it took me more than a week. Maybe it was two weeks. We weren't counting by then. City life plays dirty tricks on a cowboy. The body that was once tuned to a horse now sat astride with a stupid expression asking, "Just what the hell is this you expect me to do?"

But Chuckles was a gentle, patient partner. As we'd lope off across the sagebrush, he forgave the floppiness and miscues as we grew to learn each other. Chuckles lost his grass belly and got back into shape before I did. He breathed more easily on our daily lopes over the hills. In a short time, he'd tuned himself into a running machine.

And as my muscles and mind gradually switched over to horseback, I really began to appreciate this bay horse. I'd never ridden a horse that was as smooth through rock piles and the sage flats. He flowed over and around obstacles. And, to my everlasting shock, about a week or so later, I began to flow with him.

What happens is inexplicable and deserves a few moments' consideration. There is a memory built into the mind and the muscles that, once learned, never disappears. There comes a moment that good horsemen learn, when you cease being man and horse and become a traveling unit. When it happens, it is a wondrous thing. You can sit back and remember the feeling again and again in later years when all you ride is a pickup truck.

You learn the way the horse thinks and how he moves, and how far each leg moves on each stride and just where he'll put his feet. And a lot of it depends on how long his legs are and how flat or steep the terrain may be. You can look down, in the early stages, and know just where the right hoof will go and where the left hoof will go. Just ahead of that rock with the right, and just short of that clump of grass with the left. And later in this early stage, you'll begin to know by feel where those hind legs are going to touch down. And when those massive hindquarters give a heave up over a log, you are with him and you know it. Because you know it.

Then, after many hours in the saddle over long days, and if you have spent years riding in your youth, you can pick up once again the rhythm of the horse. Not just any horse, but this nice bay, Chuckles. No two horses will run a dodging pattern through sagebrush the same. It may look the same to someone who is watching, but not to the rider in the saddle. Each horse's way of traveling is like a fingerprint. Blindfolded, and at any gait, you will be able to tell your horse from others.

Finally, your unstretched muscles limber up and begin to fit the saddle and the horse. As this happens, you can begin to feel the horse beneath you as an extension of yourself and not an alien being whose back you are on for transportation.

Finally, when the horse is let out into a run, your muscles flex along and you sense, rather than see, the changes in the ground beneath you. When the horse strains over an obstacle, your body strains with it, shifting to put your body where it will do the horse the most good. And these reflexes happen ten times to a second, twenty or fifty times to a second until there is just one being with two brains moving through the brush, with one brain telegraphing movement to the other, and the other sending body signals to the first. And one says where you'll go, and the other says how you'll go, and the two just go and flow, like some primordial fugue, with the messages chasing each other and complementing each other and all of it making sense and a spooky kind of poetry at the same time.

That's what happens when it's good.

THIRTEEN

Are you an objective reporter?

No you aren't and neither am I. Oh, it would be fun to be one. Think of how much pride we'd take in ourselves. But all of us are flawed. We haven't spent all this time on earth (even 18 or 20 years, maybe, in your case) without coming to some private decisions. We like this. We don't like that. One political party is the only hope the nation has. The other one stinks and is leading us to disaster.

My church is the only way and guess where you're going?

I've been a reporter since 1964 and I've never met an objective reporter, nor have I ever been one. But even we flawed, biased, prejudiced reporters are able to write an objective story, and that's what counts.

The very first week on my first paper, the editor called me over and pointed to something in a regular police-beat story I'd written that showed my disdain for whatever kind of lowlife scum had just been captured by the cops.

"No one cares what you think about it!" he said,

none too gently. "Just who the hell are you?"

He crumpled up the paper (we used paper back in the olden days) and it hit the circular file. Perfect two-point play.

"You just report what happened. Let people come up with their own opinions."

Very true. I'm sure glad I learned it when I was 21. I know some TV types in their 50s who haven't had that advantage yet.

When we write about something, or someone, it is incumbent on us to say, in effect, "This is what happened." Whether we like or dislike what happened really isn't any of our business, is it?

When you get so old that you have to have help chewing your food, they'll trust you to be a columnist and express an opinion. By that time, of course, you've seen so much that you doubt all those conclusions you've drawn for the past hundred years, but at least you've been around long enough to know the libel laws. You're unlikely to step over them.

Also, we owe it to the people we write about to tell their story. Hey, that's what we went out after, right?

I have always considered it a minor triumph if my readers don't know where I stand on the hot-button issues. If they can't figure it out, good. That means I'm doing my job.

Let me give you an example. You've figured out by now that I enjoy hunting. Maybe it's the mention of all those years I spent guiding hunters in Alaska and New Mexico. Little clue there. Plus, I'm known as an outdoor writer in books as well as stories.

But when I was writing my column "Bosque Beat" for the *Albuquerque Journal*, I ran into a woman who was ardently and avidly against hunting. So I interviewed her. According to her, hunters should be snuffed out and field dressed. I smiled and asked questions and took notes.

Then I wrote her story. It was all in there. All the hate for people and love for animals. She loved the story and called me up and told me so.

And my buddies called me up and said "Have you gone NUTS?!"

I found, the very next week, a woman who was having the time of her life hunting with her husband and children. I interviewed her and wrote her story. That was my job.

A guy I'd hunted all over the state with called me up and told me he was glad I'd had a change of heart.

I hadn't. Same old heart. Same old passion for hunting. I hadn't changed a bit.

But I felt good because I'd interviewed two women who were both passionate on opposite sides of what some consider a controversy, and I'd told their stories fairly and accurately.

You'll run into situations like that, too. Remember that the story is the thing, not your opinion of the story. The person giving you an interview has every right to believe a certain way, and you have every obligation to see that their point comes across. You don't have to like it. You just have to do it.

If you do, I'll be proud of you! Go have some fun.

Also Available by Slim Randles . . .

Home Country
Drama, dreams, and laughter from America's heartland
Best Self-help/Humor Book,
2012 New Mexico-Arizona Book Awards
Best Humor Book,
2013 National Federal of Press Women Book Awards
Finalist, Best Humor Book,
2013 International Book Awards
ISBN 978-1-936744-03-9   200pp $17.95

A Cowboy's Guide to Growing Up Right
Best Self-help/Humor Book,
2011 New Mexico Book Awards
ISBN 978-1-890689-91-9 68pp $8.95

CPSIA information can be obtained at www.ICGtesting.com
Printed in the USA
LVOW06s1817070214

372804LV00002B/3/P